The
Golfer's
Two-Minute
Workout

The Golfer's Two-Minute Workout

Add 30 Yards to Your Drive in Six Weeks

PETER N. SISCO AND JOHN R. LITTLE

Foreword by Bruce Cadwell

CB
CONTEMPORARY BOOKS

Library of Congress Cataloging-in-Publication Data

Sisco, Peter.
   The golfer's two-minute workout :   add 30 yards to your drive in six
weeks / Peter N. Sisco and John R. Little ; foreword by Bruce Cadwell.
      p.   cm.
   ISBN 0-8092-2939-0
   1. Golf—Drive. 2. Muscle strength. 3. Golf—Training.   I. Little, John
R., 1960– . II. Title.
   GV979.D74S57   1998
   796.352'33—dc21   97-46832
                                                                          CIP

Cover design by Todd Petersen
Cover photograph copyright © Lori Adamski Peek/Tony Stone Images
Interior design by Precision Graphics

Published by Contemporary Books
A division of NTC/Contemporary Publishing Group, Inc.
4255 West Touhy Avenue, Lincolnwood (Chicago), Illinois 60646-1975 U.S.A.
Copyright © 1998 by Peter N. Sisco and John R. Little
Printed in the United States of America
International Standard Book Number: 0-8092-2939-0
18 17 16 15 14 13 12 11 10 9 8 7 6 5 4 3 2 1

Contents

FOREWORD

BRUCE CADWELL

I have been playing golf since the age of five or six, when I used to caddie for my dad when he played with his pals. That was over five decades ago now, and I have worked on my game for all the intervening years, sometimes with more success, sometimes less. One aspect I have always sought to improve—and most other golfers do too since it is a much ballyhooed statistic—is the distance I can drive the ball. I know that if I have a long drive off a par 5 my chances of getting on in two are greatly increased, and on a par four I might just have a wedge shot into the green. My swing is pretty consistent, and when my timing and rhythm are in sync, I can usually hit the ball a fair distance. However, I have never run across any exercise or training device that can truly improve my driving distance on a consistent basis—until now!

In a recent test conducted by the authors of this book, golfers who utilized the Golfer's Two-Minute Workout improved their average driving distance by nearly 15 yards after a mere fourteen-and-a-half minutes of total training time. One subject, age 54, after performing six workouts of only two minutes each, increased her total strength by 107 percent and lengthened her average drive by 18 yards. One of the most revolutionary aspects of this training system is that it is the shortest workout imaginable (a mere two minutes of actual training time once a week), and yet it has proved to be the most effective tool for increased strength, which, with all other parts of the swing being equal, leads to greater driving distance. I personally have used the Golfer's Two-Minute Workout in my off-season conditioning program and have enthusiastically recommended it to my friends and colleagues.

Renowned health and fitness authorities John Little and Peter Sisco have collaborated to engineer the ultimate golfer's workout. This unique system was conceived of by John Little in 1985, and its development has an interesting background. After extensively using this method with bodybuilders (all of whom became substantially stronger and more muscular), Little and Sisco tested a theory they had entertained for years, that is, the application of the Two-Minute Workout to other athletic pursuits. They postulated that, with all other aspects of his game being equal, if a golfer's muscular strength increased, would he then be able to hit the ball consistently farther? After a six-week study at Crane Creek Country Club in Boise, Idaho, involving eight experienced golfers, Little and Sisco proved the validity of their theory: every golfer in the study increased his or her muscular strength as well as the distance they could drive the ball on a consistent basis. This is great news for the average golfer who would like the slightest advantage in his game. "Average golfer" is the key term, in that this system can work for anybody. This workout requires an absolute minimum of time and equipment. With all other parts of the swing and mental game remaining constant, this one small change can result in dramatic and substantial improvement in one's game.

These are just some of the positive results that this new workout system can provide to golfers looking to improve their game. Additional health and fitness benefits were experienced by all the golfers in the test study. Abundant energy, less fatigue, greater mental focus, increased confidence, and improved appearance were simultaneous dividends, leading, naturally, to even greater rewards on the course. The Golfer's Two-Minute Workout has a synergistic effect on all aspects of the golfer's game.

Increased strength has been a neglected aspect of the amateur golfer's repertoire. Better equipment has gone a long way in helping golfers hit a longer ball, but the golfing champions of the future will have to emphasize internal changes in order to get from those clubs the extra few yards that may be the difference between being next to the pin or ten yards short of the green. I have adapted Little and Sisco's strength-training theories to my training regime for the last year and I feel it has improved my game. If you are serious about working on your game and have an extra two minutes per week, I highly recommend you give the Golfer's Two-Minute Workout a try.

Bruce Cadwell
(Ranked in the Top Ten Senior Amateurs in America
by the editors of *Golf Digest* magazine,
January 1997)

INTRODUCTION

The book you are now holding in your hands is a revolutionary one. We realize that "revolutionary" is a powerful word, usually employed to describe someone or something that defies the status quo and overthrows an established tradition or institution. The concept is generally applied to political or social issues but, occasionally, revolutionary ideas disrupt the physical sciences as well. Such is the case with the Golfer's Two-Minute Workout.

Consider the following documented results: a 31-yard increase in the distance of one subject's average drive distance and an increase of nearly 15 yards for the average subject of the study after less than 15 minutes of training time on this system; an average increase in overall body strength of 84 percent; an increase in stamina, better mental focus, balance, and superior athletic performance noted after only 15 minutes of actual training time!

In case you are wondering, no new "ultralight" clubs, radical new driving techniques, or lessons in Eastern philosophy were employed to obtain any of the above results. Would you consider such progress, and the training methods that produced them, revolutionary? Of course you would, but they are also firmly grounded in the sciences of physics and human muscle physiology.

By utilizing conventional golfing methodology, these gains would have been impossible. According to the prevailing wisdom in such matters, golf is a game of technique and mental focus—not strength. The implication of this is that the only way one can improve significantly is by redesigning or modifying one's swing or by performing a similar makeover of one's state of consciousness. And then perhaps after many months or, in some instances, years, you might—someday, somehow—be rewarded for your labors with a "little bit" of improvement in your game. You'll be relieved to learn that this popular belief has now been proven to have no basis in scientific fact.

The Golfer's Two-Minute Workout is based on a revolutionary approach to exercise and startling new research on its applications carried out in 1997 by the authors. Our unique Static Contraction training program was employed in a scientific study featuring eight golfers, aged 18 to 58. These men and women were given extremely short exercise routines consisting of only six exercises in which a weight was held motionless (instead of being pumped up and down) for a period of only 10 to 20 seconds. After a mere six weeks of training, wherein each subject trained an average of once per week, the subjects had gained over 14 yards on their average driving distance, were able to play more holes for longer periods of time without becoming fatigued, and also substantially shaped up their bodies, gaining muscle and losing body fat at the same time! What has made these results the talk of the golfing world is the fact that each workout took only two minutes to complete!

For years strength has been maligned or dismissed as being, at best, an unimportant consideration in improving the golfer's game. As a result of the data from our experiment, we now know that it is an absolutely critical factor in improving not only the golfer's overall levels of health and fitness, but in dramatically improving his game as well. Golf is a muscular game; it requires muscles to swing your club, pivot your feet, rotate your hips, and arc your swing. In fact, if you are anything less than as strong as you can be, then you will be operating, by definition, at a submaximal standard.

To this end, when a golfer wishes to add more distance or power to his game, the answer lies in increasing the strength of the muscles he must utilize. However, for years this aspect of conditioning has all but been ignored in favor of less tangible factors. In this book compelling evidence is offered to support the contention that "a stronger golfer is a better golfer," and the good news is that it takes almost no time to become a stronger golfer!

Technology has finally been brought to bear on the "physical game" of golf. With *The Golfer's Two-Minute Workout*, you now have in your hands a very potent means to not only get into tremendous shape but also to improve your game more quickly and more efficiently than with any other training method presently known.

The
Golfer's
Two-Minute
Workout

Chapter 1

WHY YOU NEED
THIS BOOK

With the purchase of this book you are in possession of new and powerful information that will propel you to your next level as a golfer. Your game is going to improve— dramatically—in many different aspects. You will feel more energetic, and your forays to the golf course will now see you with a heretofore unprecedented level of energy.

In addition, your power, i.e., your ability to hit the ball great distances, will increase to a point that will amaze you and perhaps astound your golfing partners. You will find that after utilizing this revolutionary two-minute workout, your strength levels will improve to such a high degree that you will be able to sustain your focus or "mental energy" for much longer periods, as you will no longer find that your muscles tire as quickly as before. In addition, the general fatigue you may have felt heading onto the 18th hole will be replaced with power and vigor.

Sound too good to be true? It gets better; the actual physical "cost" to you for such improvement is a mere two-minute workout, performed initially only two times per week, then just once per week. That's right, a total of only two to four minutes of training a week on this program will make you a superior golfer. How long until you see such results? To some extent, you will notice them right away, in as much as your progress should be progressive from workout to workout. Based on our test results (since dubbed "the Crane Creek Experiment," in deference to the private club at which our study was conducted), we are fully confident that you will see demonstrable progress in as little as three weeks.

We are, of course, fully aware of the fact that for years golfers who have sought to add more power to their drive and more focus to their game have been told to look to such ethereal disciplines as Zen and Taoism. These disciplines, while valid, unfortunately place the emphasis to improve one's golf game solely upon mental matters (which would be great if golf were played telepathically) rather than physical ones. It has been our experience that most golfers are operating at about 40 percent of their physical capacities. Despite this observation, there are without doubt some incredible golfers in both the pro and amateur ranks that are burning up the fairways of courses all around the world—while still operating at only 40 percent of their potential strength.

The point of this book is to help all these golfers bring their physical game up to a standard that is at least as high as their mental game, and in so doing to amplify their physical/mental capacity to levels approaching peak efficiency.

WHY A STRONGER GOLFER IS A BETTER GOLFER

It is a simple fact that, all things being equal (i.e., the same equipment and skill/technique levels), the stronger golfer is the

A STRONGER GOLFER IS ABLE TO SWING THE CLUB FASTER AND HIT THE BALL HARDER AND FARTHER.

better golfer. A stronger golfer is able to swing the club faster, hit the ball harder and farther, and better control the muscles necessary for directing the ball to its intended target, whether it be the midpoint on the fairway or the ever elusive hole-in-one. Strength is a by-product of muscles, of which every golfer from Jack Nicklaus to Tiger Woods has the same complement of six hundred. It might prove beneficial at this point to reveal to you some other things you have in common with these great golfers. For example, you and every great golfing champion who has ever lived have:

- **OVER 60,000 MILES OF BLOOD AND LYMPH VESSELS**

- **OVER THREE MILLION SWEAT GLANDS**

- **43 MAJOR JOINTS, WHICH ENABLE YOU TO MOVE**

- **A HEART THAT WEIGHS 10.5 OUNCES**

- **APPROXIMATELY 14 BILLION NERVE CELLS AND OVER 100 TRILLION OTHER CELLS, WHICH PROVIDE COMMUNICATION AMONG AND BETWEEN ALL PARTS OF THE BODY**

- **206 BONES, HALF OF WHICH ARE IN YOUR HANDS AND FEET**

- **FIVE MILLION HAIRS ON YOUR BODY, ONLY 100,000 OF WHICH ARE ON YOUR HEAD**

We mention these facts of physiology only to disabuse the reader of any notions he may have that these elite golfers were simply "born that way." The truth is we all possess the same raw materials (barring genetic handicaps, obviously) as these so-called "thoroughbreds" of the sport.

WHY GOLFERS NEED MORE STRENGTH

Muscles are the engine that drives the human machine in the game of golf and, just like a car engine, the more care and maintenance you give it, the better it performs. Given the supreme importance that your muscles play in the game of golf, it seems strange that more golfers haven't spent more time looking after their "engine." As indicated above, we each possess 600 muscles that, collectively, are responsible for allowing us to not only play the game of golf but also to simply go about our daily activities.

It's also common knowledge that if we don't make an effort to keep them strong and balanced in relationship to each other, these same muscles will slowly wither away with the passage of time. This explains why many of us see our handicaps rise as we get older. Certainly this cannot be solely attributed to a lack of neuromuscular efficiency or "technique," since the older one gets, and the more games one plays, the stronger the neuromuscular pathways laid down within the central nervous system become. This results in a greater refinement of one's swing and technical proficiency.

The decline in one's performance cannot be solely attributed to a decline in one's mental faculties either, as some of history's greatest thinkers and philosophers have made their most meritorious discoveries and insights when they were well into their autumn years, which would seem to argue the case that one's consciousness, understanding, and mental acuity actually increases with age.

The only factor that has demonstrably declined as the golfer ages is strength or health, the two terms being synonymous for our purposes (because, after all, one does not become unhealthier as they become stronger, nor healthier as they become weaker). And yet, strength training is the one activity that most golfers—particularly those who need it most—shy away from, preferring instead to compensate for their lack of strength by buying a lighter graphite club or by reading a book on "the mental game" of golf.

On the subject of a golfer's well-being, it is certainly no secret among exercise physiologists that strength training improves posture, helps prevent back pain, and is the foundation of life-long physical skill, balance, and coordination. But strength is also one of the major elements in good golf, as the other components of speed, timing, mobility, flexibility, endurance, and coordination correlate exactly with a golfer's muscular strength.

LOSE FAT—AND IMPROVE YOUR GOLF GAME!

That a golfer can actually become leaner by engaging in strength training sounds like a contradiction. After all, most golfers consider strength training useful only if one's goal is to build big, bulky, "body-beautiful" muscles, right? To lose body fat or, for you women golfers out there, to get "shapely," people are always better advised to engage in aerobics classes, aren't they? Well, evidently weight training—for years considered the weak sister of health and fitness exercise—might now usurp the throne. Recent studies have proven that strength training, performed for the express purpose of increasing one's lean body mass, can actually be more effective than aerobics in reducing your body fat levels, resulting in startling changes in one's appearance—and performance. The key to unlocking this "new you" lies in understanding the way in which muscle tissue affects your metabolism and why your body's composition is actually more important than your body's weight.

Muscle tissue, unlike fat cells, is termed "active" tissue. In other words, a certain number of calories are required simply to sustain its existence. In fact, for every pound of muscle on your body, between 50 and 100 calories are required daily simply to sustain its cellular activity. If you were to add a pound of muscle to your frame between now and your tee-off time this Friday, your body's natural metabolism would be increased by roughly 75 calories per day—even while you were completely inactive! That may not sound like much but, given the fact that there are 3,500 calories in a pound of fat tissue, if you were able to sustain that extra pound of muscle for an entire year, you would lose about eight pounds of fat from your body! Try to envision eight pounds of butter on top of your kitchen table and you will begin to get an idea of just how radical a change in appearance this would truly make. Additionally, fat serves as a friction, or brake, in between your muscle fibers, with the result that your contractile ability (i.e., the ability of your muscles to function optimally, such as when attempting to generate maximum power for a drive) is compromised by every pound of fat you carry on your frame.

The converse of the above example is also true; that is, if you were to lose a pound of muscle tissue, you would also lose 75 calories a day of energy-burning potential, with the result that these calories would now end up being stored as fatty tissue. The result would be a rather profound change in both your appearance and your performance on the golf course; only this time you would add eight pounds of fat.

A recent study revealed strength training to be more effective than aerobics for the purpose of losing body fat. Two groups of 36 men and women were compared after having completed an eight-week program. All of them consumed a reduced calorie diet made up of 20% fat, 20% protein, and 60% carbohydrates. In addition, the subjects were required to exercise three times per week for 30 minutes a session. One group combined a 15-minute total-body strength-training program with 15 minutes of aerobic exercise. The other group did 30 minutes of aerobic activity only. The results were fascinating, producing conclusions that should affect every one of us who has taken up some form of aerobic activity to not only become more proficient at our golf game but also to lose some fat. The aerobic exercise–only group lost an average of 3.2 pounds of fat, which, on the surface, appears to be a pretty impressive number for a mere eight-week time investment, until you contrast their results with what the strength training/aerobic exercise group accomplished! They lost an average of ten pounds of fat— almost three times more fat loss! It's also significant to note that this group also gained an average of two pounds of muscle per person, compared to a loss of a half a pound of muscle per person among the aerobic exercise–only group.

Knowing that all of us, from age 20 onward, will naturally lose about a half a pound of muscle per year (which results in a reduction of approximately a half percent from our resting metabolic rate), and in view of the above research information, an effective strength-training program would appear to be the most efficient route to our turning our bodies into lean, mean golfing machines, and perhaps more important, to our being able to sustain our "golfing machines" as we get older.

WOMEN GOLFERS AND THE WAR AGAINST OSTEOPOROSIS

Strength training yields another dividend, that of increased bone density. Studies have demonstrated repeatedly that physical activity increases bone mineral content. More specifically, weight bearing or resistance exercise—such as the program in this book—has been associated with greater bone density. Sports medicine practitioners have universally concluded that strength training is beneficial in the prevention of osteoporosis, a condition that largely affects postmenopausal women, in whom the density of bone decreases over time, causing the bones to become brittle and more easily fractured.

According to recent studies, osteoporosis currently afflicts some 24 million Americans. One out of every three women in her sixties (an age group that makes up 15% of our women's golf population) is estimated to suffer a fracture in the spine because of it. Theories on the treatment of osteoporosis are by no means conclusive, but it's obvious that lifestyle factors such as exercise clearly influence the development of bone strength.

An interesting fact regarding the significance of resistance on our bones was brought to light by, of all people, the renowned aerobics guru Dr. Kenneth Cooper, who recently wrote:

Along with many other exciting revelations from the NASA space program, the effect of weightlessness on bone mass reinforced the belief that exercise is important in the maintenance of bone strength. Using techniques which allowed scientists to measure the bone density of the astronauts of Skylab 4 both before and after space flight, it was discovered that weightlessness caused a marked loss of bone strength. In the absence of the pull of gravity, the bones were no longer required to support the weight of the body. As a consequence, the bones began to deteriorate rapidly. The calcium that was lost from the bones was eliminated from the body through the kidneys in such large amounts that there was actually concern that the astronauts might develop kidney stones in space! NASA's original plans for providing exercise for astronauts in space had centered around providing aerobic exercise to maintain cardiovascular fitness, which can easily be done in zero gravity. They are now working to devise forms of strength training that can be performed in order to protect the astronauts from muscle and bone deterioration.[*]

---

[*]*Cooper, Kenneth H., M.D., M.P.H., with Sydney Lou Bonnick, M.D., "Aerobic Exercise, Strength Training, and Bone Mass," published in* The New Fitness Formula of the '90s, *(Excelsior, Minn.: National Exercise for Life Institute, 1990).*

THE OVER-FORTY BENEFIT FOR "SENIOR" GOLFERS—THE HGH CONNECTION

If you're impressed so far at the benefits provided by strength training in the above scenarios, just wait until you read the results of a study carried out in 1990. Human Growth Hormone (HGH) was administered to twelve hormone-deficient men (aged 61 to 81) for a period of six months. After the six months of HGH injections, these men were found to have increased their percentage of lean body weight (i.e., muscle mass) by 9%—while simultaneously dropping 14% of their body fat! The most incredible component of this study was the fact that these individuals made this spectacular progress without exercising! Not only did these individuals increase their strength and muscle mass, but some even proclaimed a renewed interest in sex. Most claimed that they had "never felt better." The researchers who conducted this experiment later declared that the physiological reversal these individuals displayed was comparable to their having shed 10 to 20 years of age.

So what is so magical about this HGH? Well, as touched upon, HGH is an acronym for Human Growth Hormone, a naturally occurring substance in the human body. We produce less growth hormone in our fifties, sixties, and seventies than we do in our twenties. We know growth hormone helps to burn fat and build muscles and to improve metabolism. Increased levels of growth hormone may result in substantial benefits, including a healthier heart (as HGH lowers cholesterol levels in the blood and may further serve to keep fat from collecting around the abdomen, thereby reducing the risk of heart disease), a stronger immune system, quicker healing response, and an increased sex drive. But it is growth hormone's ability to build muscle mass and reduce fat that is especially striking. Research reveals that HGH affects the body's metabolism, causing it to burn fat to meet energy demands while converting the building block proteins to muscle.

Not to rain so early on the HGH parade, but there does exist a darker side to this "wonder drug." The problems associated with HGH injections center around determining just where the fine line exists between an "ideal" dose and an overdose (and this would appear to be a highly individual thing), as too much of this apparent good thing can produce the following list of problems: carpal tunnel syndrome, osteoporosis, diabetes, arthritis, and heat intolerance. But let's not throw the baby out with the bath water; the problems, as they exist, do so only by receiving overdoses of the synthetic version of this hormone.

What if we could secrete more of this wonderful hormone naturally? What if we could have the benefits of an increased amount of HGH coursing through our bodies—which would serve to stave off the aging process, burn fat, build muscle mass, and make us stronger golfers—without any of the problems associated with potential overdoses and injections of its synthetic derivatives? Well, obviously, it would be great. And greater still is the fact that we can accomplish this. How? Through high-intensity exercise such as weight training or sprinting. If we consider this point a minute, heavy overload training, the kind that would see you unable to continue holding a weight past the 20-second mark, would obviously involve the use of a maximal contraction. And the more tension generated by the muscle (i.e., the greater the contraction), the more HGH we should be able to secrete naturally. Static Contraction training, as you shall soon see, provides a method that allows you to generate the highest possible intensity in your workouts and, by so doing, ensures that you're stimulating natural production of your HGH with every workout, thereby making you a leaner and stronger golfer from week to week.

THE GOLFER'S TWO-MINUTE WORKOUT AND STRESS RELIEF

Many people take up the sport of golf with the mistaken notion that simply "whacking a few golf balls around the course" will provide them with some form of stress relief. Then they wonder why, when they miss the ball or become winded after only six holes, their blood pressure levels are only getting higher. There's no better way to relieve stress than properly conducted strength-training exercise wherein you perform one intense exercise and then have a brief respite until you perform your next exercise.

Obviously total fitness includes the mind as well as the body, and the Golfer's Two-Minute Workout is also useful as a means to relieve mental stress. The late stress research pioneer Dr. Hans Selye wrote at length about how mental stress, if left unchecked, can quickly lead to physical malfunctions. Selye maintained that everything from heart attacks to alcoholism and obesity can be caused by stress, and that the relief of such stress can go a long way toward the elimination of such problems.

It's obvious that skeletal muscle strength is integral to our level of proficiency in golf, but our mental well-being also plays a major role in our overall performance. Not that this is a novel concept by any means. The "mind/body" relationship was first brought forth by the Greeks and later by the Romans as the "ideal" we should strive for, with their concept of "mens sana in corpore sano" (a sound mind in a sound body). Wilhelm Reich later concluded that physical problems such as asthma, rheumatism, hypertension, and ulcers were also often the result of chronic mental anxiety. Selye's studies from the 1930s added migraine headaches, obesity, heart attacks, and neck pain to Reich's list of stress-related physical maladies. With overcrowded psychiatrists' offices and more people on "stress" medications than ever before, there can be little doubt that the "stress of life" is difficult to handle for many individuals and poses a real problem in their day-to-day existence.

But what exactly is stress and, more important, how can we take steps to remove or at least lessen its presence in our lives? According to Selye, stress can be defined as "the nonspecific response of the body to any demand." The body's reaction to this is what Selye termed the General Adaptation Syndrome, or GAS: a three-tiered response that begins with an "alarm stage," is followed by a "stage of resistance," and concludes with a "stage of exhaustion." The stress itself can cause internal chemical reactions, which include the release of adrenaline, a faster heart rate, faster reflex speed, muscle tenseness, and accelerated thought processes. Selye's research indicated that our bodies react exactly the same way to stress, whether it's in the form of pleasure, success, failure, or depression. Both "good" and "bad" life situations evidently cause what the body perceives as "stress," and everyone is under some degree of stress even when asleep.

In other words, stress is the rate of daily wear and tear of our existence. Its effects, however, depend on how we adapt to it and how we're able to dissipate its accumulation of repressed energy. Our General Adaptation Syndrome is always in operation, often on an emergency basis, but the physical outlets for its dissipation are not built in. And it's becoming clear that these dammed-up emotions have to be released on a regular basis if we are to stay mentally healthy and become better golfers.

Exercise is the most productive means of release in this regard. Although most active exercises can reduce tension levels in the body, strength training appears to be unique in that it can be pinpointed to the precise area where the stress is located, for example, in the neck, stomach, shoulders, or back. Exercise can provide immediate relief for tension in these areas as well as remove the general feeling of lethargy that results from our daily wear-and-tear encounters. All of these life-enhancing benefits do not have to come slowly. In fact, they can come quite rapidly and consistently if certain kinesiological and physiological principles are acknowledged and specific exercises are performed. These factors are the cornerstones of the Golfer's Two-Minute Workout.

THE BENEFITS

The Golfer's Two-Minute Workout was designed to provide golfers of all levels with a three-fold dividend:

1. TO GENERATE INCREASED STRENGTH IN THE MUSCLES USED BY GOLFERS

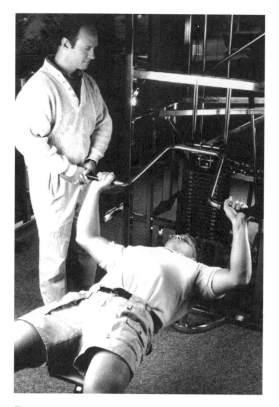

DONE PROPERLY, THIS EXERCISE IS COMPLETED, WITHOUT ANY UP-AND-DOWN MOTION, IN ABOUT THE TIME IT TAKES TO READ THIS CAPTION.

2. TO MINIMIZE TRAINING TIME NEEDED TO ACHIEVE THESE STRENGTH INCREASES

3. TO MEASURE THE EFFECTS OF INCREASED STRENGTH ON THE DISTANCE A GOLFER CAN HIT A DRIVE

The Golfer's Two-Minute Workout is unique in that it represents a genuine innovation in the realm of exercise. There has never been a book like this for the simple fact that there has never been a training system like this—ever. And, more important, the results of the Golfer's Two-Minute Workout are documented as being powerfully effective in accomplishing its objective of creating better, stronger golfers who are able to consistently hit the ball longer distances and to achieve this improvement with an absolute minimum of exercise time.

Chapter 2

THE GREAT GOLF
EXPERIMENT

From the beginning, it was our intention to design an experiment
that would test the benefits of strength training in a way that was
most beneficial to golfers. Our previous study with Static
Contraction training was performed on forty experienced bodybuilders. It was designed to measure parameters of interest to
bodybuilders, such as inches gained on biceps and shoulders,
increases in weight lifted, pounds of muscle gained, and pounds
of fat lost. We knew from conducting the study with
bodybuilders that the strength results for golfers would be very
substantial, and we wanted to determine how substantial
strength increases would transfer into usable strength for golfers.

The parameters of this study were simple and to the point. We would randomly select a group of golfers from a broad range of ages and abilities and measure their driving distance before and after six weeks of training. The subjects were taken to a local driving range to perform thirty consecutive drives so as to obtain a meaningful average distance. Recognizing that there can be considerable variation in the distance of a drive, even with the same golfer on the same day, it was decided that taking an average of thirty drives would provide a meaningful average.

Accurately measuring the average distance of drives per subject can be more complicated than one might imagine. One of the first things we noticed was that when a golfer is asked how far he hits a ball he will almost invariably tell you his best distance on his best day under ideal circumstances. This, of course, is human nature and certainly nothing peculiar to golfers. Taking an average of thirty consecutive drives yielded the broad range of data that would provide a meaningful number for comparison. We also noted that people at a driving range often don't pay attention to where the beginning measurement should be taken. It is a common practice to move the physical starting position forward and backward so as not to cause excessive wear on one area of grass. Consequently, when a person hits a ball out to the 200-yard marker, he may not be aware that he is actually teeing off 10, 12, or 15 yards ahead of the starting line. Of course, this would mean that his true distance would really be 190, 188, or 185 yards.

This inaccuracy is further compounded by trying to determine exactly where a ball has stopped from 600 feet or more away. Our test subjects teed off from the number one position at the driving range, which is to say they were as close to the mesh fence as possible. The observers were just outside the fence and positioned downrange so as to be alongside the exact position where each ball stopped rolling. These observers recorded the distance of each ball that made it downrange. It should be noted that balls that were hooked into the fence were not counted. The intention was to measure the distance of balls that actually made it downrange. As the golfers who participated in this study were all quite proficient, it was a rare occurrence for a ball to go into the fence.

The data from these drives became the baseline for improvement, if any, of each golfer when he or she returned after six weeks of performing our specialized, two-minute workouts. The subjects were recruited from a local private golf club, Crane Creek Country Club in Boise, Idaho. We deliberately selected four male and four female subjects. Their profiles are as follows:

STUDY SUBJECTS

Mike M., Sr., was already quite strong at the beginning of this study but made substantial improvement in very few workouts. Mike's intensity surpassed everyone else's on the study. His effort and concentration in lifting what soon became enormously heavy weights was, we are sure, a very significant factor in his end results.

Mike M., Jr., is the son of Mike M., Sr., and showed the same intense effort in his workouts. Mike is also on his high school swimming and wrestling teams and was getting regular exercise in conjunction with those sports. He has golfed "on and off for twelve years" and plays about four times per year. It should be noted that Mike does not consider himself to be proficient with a driver, so a 6-iron was used for both his "before" and "after" drives.

Paul R. skied for the University of Denver for four years. He won the NCAA slalom and the NCAA combined skiing events

STUDY SUBJECT STATS

	AGE	HEIGHT	WEIGHT	YEARS GOLFING	HANDICAP
MIKE M., SR.	58	5′8″	195	44	12
MIKE M., JR.	18	5′8″	135	10	N/A
PAUL R.	51	5′7″	150	40	11
STEVE H.	50	5′9″	156	7	18
BONNIE H.	48	5′5″	117	12	19
JOYCE L.	49	5′ 5½″	138	20	16
KATHY M.	55	5′ 7½″	133	20	24
LAURA G.	54	5′0″	120	20	24

and then went on to ski on the NOR-AM circuit and the World Cup circuit. He was on the "B" team for the Olympic Games. Paul still performs aerobics three times per week and mountain bikes a couple of times a week or works out with weights. Paul's leg strength was enormous from the beginning of this study and, with an 11 handicap, we felt it would be most challenging to show any improvement in a person who was already an excellent golfer with strength and conditioning that was far above average.

Steve H. maintained an aerobic exercise program that included up to 40 miles per week of treadmill running in addition to the intense strength training program we had designed for him. This provided another difficult challenge for our study, as creating an increase in strength at the same time that the body is attempting to adapt to and cope with a 40-mile-a-week aerobic regimen is most challenging. Also, Steve had been exercising regularly with weights before beginning our program, which meant he had already seen some strength gains.

Bonnie H. is a mother of three who describes herself as having "been working out with weights for at least 20 years, pretty religiously. I have been pretty athletic all my life." Bonnie was very fit from the beginning of this study and, like Steve, had been working out with weights to improve her strength before beginning the Golfer's Two-Minute Workout. These factors make it much more difficult to manifest improvement.

Joyce L., too, was very fit and had lifted weights in the past. She had considerable strength to begin with, particularly in her legs, and was quite enthusiastic about performing exercises to further increase her strength. Her very respectable 16 handicap and 20 years of golf experience posed another challenge to this program. Golfers at this level normally have to accept improvement in very small increments, if at all.

Kathy M. was very enthusiastic about this program. Despite being in excellent condition to begin with, she had the largest increase in overall strength gains of anyone on the program.

Laura G. had not performed any strength-training exercise in the past and had some apprehension about lifting heavy weights. Also, Laura and Joyce had planned an overseas trip that fell in the latter half of the six weeks of this study. Consequently, they performed fewer workouts than the other subjects and had more time off between their last workout and the final measurements of their driving distance. As we will see, this had a very interesting result.

TRAINING TIME

With the data in hand of how each golfer performed at the driving range, the next step was to design a workout that involved the absolute minimum of exercise time and to measure the effects of that exercise as it related to driving distance. Twelve exercises were selected that would target the exact muscle groups most used by golfers (see Chapter 4). The training was divided into two separate workouts, each

AVERAGE DRIVE DISTANCE AT BEGINNING OF STUDY

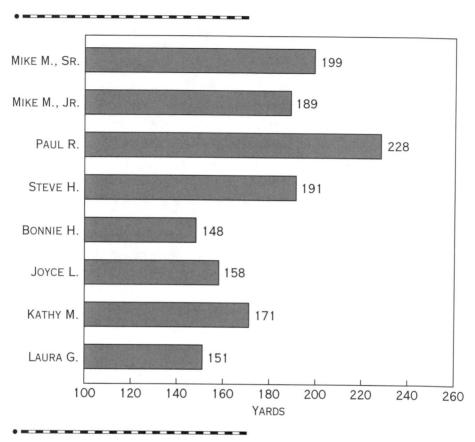

containing six of the twelve exercises. The exercises were performed for 10 to 20 seconds each per exercise. This literally means that the amount of exercise in each workout was between 60 and 120 seconds!

This is most noteworthy, as traditional and conventional strength training would have a golfer performing three to five sets of 10 to 15 repetitions each for every muscle group. Workouts of this nature often take 60 to 90 minutes to complete. As you will see, the benefits of longer strength-training workouts are not commen-

TRAINING TIME OF GOLFER'S TWO-MINUTE WORKOUT VS. CONVENTIONAL TRAINING

	BENCH PRESS	LAT PULLDOWN	SHOULDER PRESS	LEG EXTENS.	LEG CURL	WEIGHTED CRUNCH	TOTAL TIME (MIN.)
GOLFER'S TWO-MINUTE WORKOUT (15 SEC. AVERAGE PER EXERCISE)	0.25	0.25	0.25	0.25	0.25	0.25	**1.5**
CONVENTIONAL TRAINING (3 SETS OF 12 REPS + 1 MIN. BETWEEN SETS)	6.5	6.5	6.5	6.5	6.5	6.5	**39.0**

GOLFER'S TWO-MINUTE WORKOUT (1 WORKOUT PER WEEK)	**1.5**
CONVENTIONAL TRAINING (3 WORKOUTS PER WEEK)	**117.0**

surate with the time invested, to say the least. In fact, we now have conclusive data that proves that a Static Contraction training program involving one to two minutes of exertion has the same muscle-stimulating and strength-building benefits as one hour of conventional weight training. This is not a statement we ask you to take on faith. We do not even ask you to accept the data presented in this book on faith. We are hopeful that you will use the training program described in this book to duplicate the results for yourself. We have total confidence in the reproducibility of these results, as we have already seen it done in more than one thousand people.

The difference in magnitude of time invested is so dramatic that it is difficult to comprehend. The fact is that the difference depicted in the graph is actually *understated*. The conventional training program that is used for comparison

TRAINING TIME OF GOLFER'S TWO-MINUTE WORKOUT VS. CONVENTIONAL TRAINING

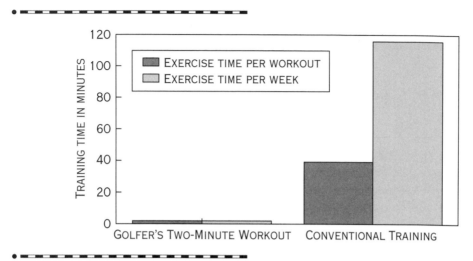

purposes is actually quite abbreviated from what would be typical. A more common routine would involve two, three, or even four exercises per body part. For example, the recommended shoulder exercises might be front barbell raises, followed by lateral dumbbell raises, followed by a shoulder press. The recommended chest exercises might be dumbbell flys, followed by an incline bench press, followed by a flat bench press. These more typical routines would make a conventional workout 300% longer than what is depicted in the above comparisons.

If that is not dramatic enough, in the course of conducting this study we determined that a per-exercise time of 20 seconds may have been more than necessary, and that a frequency of even once per week could be more frequent than necessary for intense Static Contraction training. In other words, the amount of time depicted in the graph for conventional training should be greater, and the amount of time for optimal Static Contraction training should probably be reduced! How is it even possible to design a workout involving six exercises that takes only one to two minutes to complete? Certainly it has never been done before. And given these ultralow amounts of time for muscle activity, would it be possible to see any gains whatsoever in strength? And if there were any strength gains, would they convert into measurable increases in driving distances on the golf course?

Chapter 3

A Breakthrough in Training

The increases in strength garnered from the relatively few workouts performed by these subjects was most impressive. Below is a chart indicating the strength increases seen in the test subjects. Please note that the percentages are based on a very conservative comparison of strength measurement. For example, if a subject was able to hold 100 pounds in a leg extension for 20 seconds at the beginning of the study and was by the end of the study able to hold 200 pounds for 20 seconds, the increase in strength is measured to be 100%. However, there is a paradox in the measurement of human strength.

PERCENTAGE INCREASE IN STRENGTH
PER MUSCLE GROUP

	W/O	TOTAL TIME (MIN.)	CHEST	LATS	SHLDRS	QUADS	HAMS	ABS	LOWER BACK	CALF	TRICEPS	BICEPS	FOREARM (FLEXORS)	FOREARM (EXTENSORS)	OVERALL
M ke M., Sr.	7	14.8	48%	47%	52%	57%	129%	57%	41%	52%	70%	50%	38%	80%	60%
M ke M., Jr.	8	17.8	48%	129%	52%	129%	64%	71%	62%	106%	200%	100%	57%	80%	91%
Paul R.	9	23.4	63%	47%	64%	100%	104%	233%	45%	42%	100%	67%	43%	100%	84%
Steve H.	8	17.2	55%	43%	27%	90%	67%	100%	50%	35%	75%	30%	33%	67%	56%
Bonnie H.	5	10.5	70%	33%	75%	73%	43%	300%	50%	33%	150%	50%	100%	75%	88%
Joyce L.	4	8.0	33%	50%	43%	62%	36%	100%	55%	50%	200%	63%	117%	67%	73%
Kathy M.	6	11.9	93%	78%	87%	91%	100%	200%	80%	33%	140%	133%	133%	150%	110%
Laura G.	6	12.1	50%	57%	53%	89%	83%	300%	86%	62%	125%	83%	175%	125%	107%
AVERAGE	6.6	14.5	58%	60%	57%	86%	78%	170%	58%	51%	133%	72%	87%	93%	84%

Avg. Time
Per Workout   2.2

THE PARADOX OF HUMAN STRENGTH

In the realm of physics, being able to statically hold 100 pounds for 20 seconds is also equivalent to holding 200 pounds for 10 seconds. Since the weight is doubled but the time is cut in half, the net amount of work done is equal. As a practical matter, however, a person who can support 100 pounds for 20 seconds can probably not support 200 pounds for 10 seconds and can certainly not support 400 pounds for 5 seconds, which is also the same amount of work. This example quickly demonstrates how weight has a far greater importance in the human equation than does time.

We have performed some measurements to examine this phenomena and have determined that the significance of weight is approximately (very approximately) x squared (x^2) compared to time. That is to say, if 100 pounds held for 20 seconds represents one unit of muscular output, then 200 pounds for 20 seconds represents four units of muscular output. Stated another way, if you can hold 200 pounds statically for 20 seconds before having to lower the weight, you can probably hold 100 pounds statically for about 80 seconds before having to lower the weight.

You may test this at any time in the gym. Just select a weight for a given exercise, the leg extension for example, which you can only hold for 20 seconds. Next, select one half of that weight and time how long you can hold it statically. Instead of being able to hold it twice as long (as it is half the weight) you will be able to hold it for three, four, or five times as long. Understanding this principle only serves to make the strength gains made by the test subjects even more significant. However, for the purposes of reporting strength increases, which are of secondary interest to golfers compared to driving distances, we have used a straight line percentage, which simplifies the analysis of these increases but considerably understates increases in the true magnitude of metabolic muscular output.

AVERAGE INCREASE IN STRENGTH BY MUSCLE GROUP

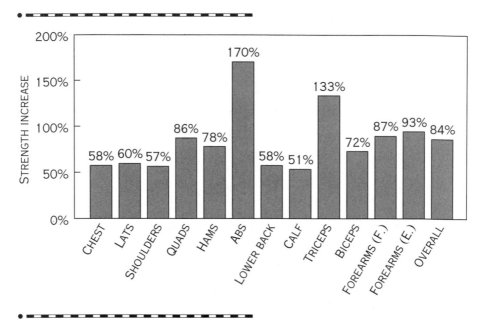

It is most significant that all of the subjects got stronger in all of the muscle groups, which points to the universality of this form of training. There are no mixed results in this data; 100% of the subjects got stronger in 100% of the targeted muscle groups. The only variance is in the degree of adaptation. This is expected in any form of metabolic adaptation. For example, eight people placed in intense sunlight for an hour will all manifest an adaptation in the form of skin darkening; however, some will tan mildly, others darkly, and others will burn.

STRENGTH INCREASES BY MUSCLE GROUP

The increases in strength are quite significant, to say the least. On average, the muscle group with the smallest increase was the calves at 51%. An increase of 51% is considered very substantial, however, particularly in light of the fact that this muscle was exercised only 3.3 times over six weeks. It should also be noted that golfers, who typically do a lot of walking, generally have a high degree of strength in their legs to begin with.

The abdominal muscles and the triceps showed very dramatic increases of 170% and 133%, respectively. This may be due to the fact that the abdominal muscles also perform work when doing biceps curls and shoulder presses, acting as stabilizer muscles during these exercises. Likewise the triceps receive substantial overload during bench presses and shoulder presses as well as during triceps pressdowns. These results point to the benefit of using compound exercises whenever possible. Compound exercises involve using several muscles or muscle groups for a single movement or, in our case, a static hold. There is an inherent efficiency in this, since it allows one exercise to perform the job of two or three separate exercises. This is an enormous benefit when trying to design an efficient workout.

The category of "Overall" represents an average of the twelve targeted muscle groups. The subjects averaged an 84% increase in their overall strength. This was accomplished with 14.5 minutes of exercise spread over six weeks! There has never been a more efficient form of strength training exercise than this. Remember that a conventional workout would have the trainee performing three sets of twelve repetitions for each of these muscle groups. That alone is 39 minutes of muscle overload. Further, conventional training would prescribe three workouts per week for the six weeks, meaning that you would spend about 100 times more time exercising your muscles! For what? Do you think you would get *more than* 84% stronger overall? You wouldn't. The fact is that even the minimal amount of training performed by our subjects began to generate overtraining.

LESS IS MORE

The four men in the study averaged eight workouts over a six-week period. The women averaged 5.25 workouts over the same

STRENGTH GAINS COMPARED
TO FREQUENCY OF WORKOUTS

MEN			
	WORKOUTS	TIME (MIN.)	GAIN IN STRENGTH
MIKE M., SR.	7	14.8	60%
MIKE M., JR.	8	17.8	91%
PAUL R.	9	23.4	84%
STEVE H.	8	17.2	56%
AVERAGE	8	18.3	73%
WOMEN			
BONNIE H.	5	10.5	88%
JOYCE L.	4	8.0	73%
KATHY M.	6	11.9	110%
LAURA G.	6	12.1	107%
AVERAGE	5.25	10.6	95%

six weeks. This lead to the women performing only 58% of the actual exercise time that the men performed (an average of 10.6 minutes over six weeks compared to 18.3 minutes for the men). Yet the women increased their overall strength by 95%, compared to 73% for the men. Why?

It could be argued that the men already had a higher level of strength and that they could not be expected to achieve as high a percentage of improvement as the women. However, the men were not engaged in any more productive strength training than the women were before this study and consequently had about as much room for improvement as the women. Furthermore, men have much higher testosterone levels than women and would normally be expected to manifest strength gains faster. Yet the women substantially outpaced the men's improvement while on the identical program—except that they trained less often. We are confident that if the men had trained less frequently than they did

REASON TO SMILE: WHILE THE WOMEN IN THIS STUDY (LEFT TO RIGHT, KATHY, BONNIE, LAURA, AND JOYCE) PERFORMED ONLY 58% OF THE EXERCISE TIME OF THE MEN IN THE STUDY, THEY STILL AVERAGED A WHOPPING 95% INCREASE IN OVERALL STRENGTH, COMPARED TO THE MEN'S 73% INCREASE.

(which only averaged 1.3 times per week), they would have seen even better results. Again, the relevance of this discovery is very dramatic when it is compared to conventional training, which would have prescribed three workouts per week, each with a duration more than 3,000% longer.

INTENSITY VS. DURATION

It is a fact of human physiology that the more intense the muscular output is, the shorter the duration for which it can be sustained. This is what is known as an inverse relationship.

INTENSITY VS. DURATION OF MUSCULAR OUTPUT

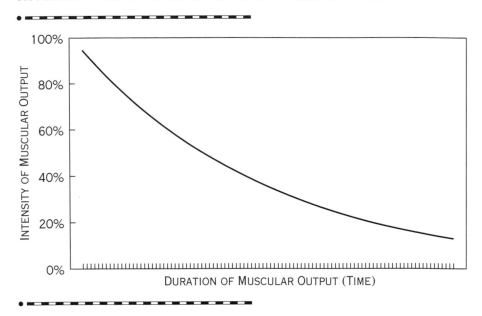

For duration to increase, intensity must decrease and vice versa. Muscles increase their strength, power, and size in response to the intensity of muscular output. Intensity is the dominant factor by far. That is why a sprinter's leg muscles are always bigger and stronger than a marathoner's leg muscles.

It logically follows that to exploit this characteristic of human physiology to the maximum, exercises designed to increase strength should be as intense as possible. Duration actually becomes an excellent yardstick in this endeavor. By definition, the longer an exercise lasts, the lower its intensity. Therefore by deliberately selecting weights that are sufficiently heavy to permit muscles to be capable of holding them for only 10 to 20 seconds of duration, we are absolutely ensuring maximal intensity. If we used weights that we could hold for 60 to 90 seconds, for example, the intensity of the muscular output would be greatly reduced.

The Golfer's Two-Minute Workout involves the absolute minimum of duration and the absolute maximum of intensity. That is why it is so effective—and so revolutionary.

In Chapter 4 you will see how we designed a training program to meet these requirements and deliver the results golfers need.

Chapter 4

CRANE CREEK ASSISTANT
PROFESSIONAL, JIM BROWN

THE TWELVE BEST EXERCISES FOR GOLFERS— THE GENERAL ROUTINE

CRANE CREEK ASSISTANT
PROFESSIONAL, JIM BROWN

It's vitally important to select exercises that allow you to utilize a weight that is heavy enough to activate the maximum number of a given muscle's fibers while in the fully contracted position. Exercises must be selected for the Golfer's Two-Minute Workout that enable a targeted muscle group to be fully loaded and contracted maximally for a 10- to 20-second time period. The list of exercises on the next page includes those exercises that have been found to be the best for the purpose of stimulating

EXERCISES AND TARGETED MUSCLE GROUPS

	EXERCISE	MUSCLE GROUP TARGETED
1.	BENCH PRESSES	PECTORALS, ANTERIOR DELTOIDS, TRICEPS
2.	LAT PULLDOWNS	LATISSIMUS DORSI
3.	SHOULDER PRESSES	DELTOIDS, TRICEPS, TRAPEZIUS
4.	LEG EXTENSIONS	QUADRICEPS
5.	LEG CURLS	HAMSTRINGS
6.	WEIGHTED CRUNCHES	ABDOMINALS
7.	NAUTILUS LOWER-BACK	ERECTOR SPINAE (LUMBAR)
8.	TOE PRESSES	GASTROCNEMIUS (CALF)
9.	TRICEPS PRESSDOWNS	TRICEPS
10.	CABLE CURLS	BICEPS
11.	WRIST CURLS	FLEXORS OF THE FOREARMS
12.	REVERSE WRIST CURLS	EXTENSORS OF THE FOREARMS

maximum muscle fiber involvement in a targeted muscle group and, hence, maximum muscle growth.

The selected exercises place a constant stress or tension on the targeted muscle groups from beginning to end and are, therefore, the most productive exercises possible. Remember, there are no repetitions involved in this program; you're to gauge your progress solely in terms of the amount of weight you are holding statically and the number of seconds you can do so. In the Golfer's Two-Minute Workout, one "set" takes between 10 and 20 seconds to perform, but the intensity is always of the highest order, thus allowing for greater strength stimulation to take place.

FREQUENCY OF TRAINING

When beginning this program it is possible, but not necessary, to perform workouts twice per week (e.g., Monday and Thursday). However, it is counterproductive to continue twice per week for more than two or three weeks. The reason for this has to do with the progressively increasing nature of the overload of each workout. When you are a beginner, your muscles are not capable of performing enormous amounts of work, which means that the metabolic waste products produced during exercise can be "cleaned up" in relatively short order by organs such as your liver and kidneys. As your strength increases—and it will—you will begin performing workouts from which your body will require several days to fully recover. Most people make the mistake of scheduling a workout right in the middle of this recovery stage. Such workouts are a waste of time, as the body will not generate new growth while still trying to recover. Furthermore, such workouts just dig a deeper metabolic hole from which your liver, kidneys, etc., must recover. Not only is this the reason that most people who lift weights never see much tangible progress over the months and years, it is also the reason most people quit going to the gym, as they grow fatigued to the point of losing all motivation. That loss of motivation is just your brain's way of keeping you from giving your body too much work from which to recover.

You can stay on a one-workout-per-week schedule for as long as you make steady progress. As soon as your progress slows or ceases it is time to change to one workout every ten days, followed by one workout every two weeks. The focus of your strategy should be to make progress with every workout rather than to maintain a preconceived schedule that may or may not result in productive workouts. If, at some point in the future, you can only make progress if you train just once every five or six weeks, then so be it. For perhaps 10–15% of you reading this book, such will be the case.

These twelve exercises are broken down into two separate workouts, simply called Workout A and Workout B. To be clear, when we say one workout per week it means only Workout A *or* Workout B, not both of them in the same week. So a typical month might see you doing Workout A on the 7th, B on the 14th, A again on the 21st, and B again on the 28th.

If you are worried that such a schedule is far less than what you have been used to with conventional strength training, please note that the women in this study averaged 0.875 workouts per week (that's less than once per week) and saw, on average, a 95% increase in their overall strength and, on average, a 15-yard increase in their drives.

Please remember that more is not better. The women in the above example would not have done twice as well if they had trained twice as often. This study and others we have conducted all show that increased training frequency results in poorer performance. The men in this study performed 1.3 workouts per week but improved their overall strength by "only" 73%. Getting three or four haircuts a week won't speed up your hair growth and performing the Golfer's Two-Minute Workout three or four times a week will not speed up your muscle growth.

TIME KEEPING

As the concept of "progressive overload" is critical to generating muscular hypertrophy, it is necessary to have a simple but accurate means to ensure progress. The Golfer's Two-Minute Workout uses a time bracket of 10 to 20 seconds of hold time. The idea is to select a weight that is sufficiently heavy as to make it impossible for you to hold for more than 10 seconds. When you exceed 10 seconds the weight begins to descend and, for all your effort, you can not hold it. That completes the exercise. As soon as the weight begins to descend, stop counting the seconds. The next time you perform the same workout your goal is to increase the hold time with the same amount of weight to beyond 10 seconds. Perhaps you will

THE GOLFER'S TWO-MINUTE WORKOUT USES A TIME BRACKET OF 10 TO 20 SECONDS OF HOLD TIME.

achieve 13, 16, or 18 seconds. As soon as you are able to hold the weight for 20 seconds, however, you should not attempt an increase in time but should instead increase the weight to an amount sufficient to once again only be held for 10 seconds. Then the cycle repeats.

For example, you might start your bench press with 150 pounds and hold it for 11 seconds. Next time you perform the bench press you achieve, say, a 19-second hold; that's close enough so that next time you increase the weight to 170 pounds and hold it for, say, 9 seconds. When you are able to hold the 170 pounds for 20 seconds, you might increase the weight to 190 or 200 pounds in order to get your time back down to ten seconds.

Also, remember that the 10 to 20 seconds is not sacrosanct. You might select too heavy a weight and only hold it 7 seconds or so. That's okay. Just mark it down on your log sheet and try to hold it longer next time. Likewise you may progress faster than anticipated and jump from 15 seconds one workout to 30 seconds the next workout with the same weight. When this happens, just select a heavier weight right away (during the same workout) to see what you need in order to get back down to 10 seconds. Mark that weight in your log so you know the right starting point for next time.

DETERMINING PROGRESS

Eventually, if you are like most people, you will reach a point where you make progress in some, but not all, exercises in a workout. This is nearly always caused by one of two forms of overtraining, localized or systemic.

If you are experiencing localized overtraining, it means that you have an individual muscle or muscle group that will not progress as fast as the rest of your muscles. For example, you may find that all of your weights and times have gone up except for your hamstrings during leg curls. The thing to do in this case is to leave the leg curls exercise off your workout next time around, which means you would do five exercises instead of six. If you have two lagging muscle groups, leave both exercises off your next identical (i.e., A or B) workout.

If, however, you have three or more exercises in which you are not making progress, you are probably suffering from systemic overtraining. In this case you should skip your very next workout entirely and adjust your training frequency to space all your workouts further apart. For example, suppose your workouts are spaced one week apart, but suddenly today you notice that you did not increase your weights on three out of six exercises. If today is the 7th, your next workout would be on the 14th. Skip the workout on the 14th. Perform the workout on the 21st and schedule the next workout for the 31st, ten days later. Adjust your frequency so that you now work out on the 10th, 20th, and 30th of the month. This should put you back on the road to steady progress. If you again achieve large gains in strength that cause overtraining on this schedule, adjust your frequency to the 1st and 15th of the month. Again, to be clear, such a schedule would mean performing workout A on the 1st and workout B on the 15th. This, believe it or not, is a schedule that many hundreds of people we know are using today.

STRONG-RANGE EXERCISES

All the exercises in this program are intended to be performed in the strongest range. For example, in performing a static bench press you could hold the bar one inch off your chest, five inches off your chest, or as far as you could reach. The strongest range, however, is to hold the weight just one or two inches from "lock out," or maximum reach. When the bar is locked out it is actually the bones that are supporting much of the weight and not the muscles. For this reason you must always ensure that you are just out of the lock-out position so that the muscles in question are performing all of the work.

In the above example, holding the weight one inch from your chest is the weakest range of motion and also the most prone to causing injury. The strongest range is the least prone to causing injury. However, once the weight is locked out you lose most of the muscle-building benefit. A readily seen example of lock out occurs when a person stands at attention. In this configuration his leg bones can support him for hours. If, however, he were to put a two-inch bend in his knees, he would shift the work of standing from his bones to his muscles. Within minutes his legs would be fatigued and shaking.

By definition, the strongest range—for every exercise—is the point where you can hold the most weight. Holding the most weight means the maximum muscle fiber use, which in turn means maximum growth stimulation. This also means that the exertion is maximal—you should be grunting and groaning in order to hold such a weight. The duration is very short, so the intensity must be very high. If you can chat with your training partner during the 10 to 20 seconds, you are using too light a weight. Holding a light or moderate weight for 10 seconds is virtually useless and will not meet your objectives.

There are two safe ways to get a heavy weight into the position of your strongest range of motion. You can have a training partner or assistant lift or help you lift the weight into position, or you can adjust the weight so that it is in the correct position when you start.

Having another person lift the weight is simple. He simply provides the extra horsepower to get the weight out of your weak range and into your strong range *and* helps you again when the weight has to be lowered. Make sure your partner realizes that when the 10 to 20 seconds has expired he needs to help lower the weight back to the rest position. Make sure he doesn't simply "drop" the weight into your fully contracted position, as the sudden shock to the joint of articulation could prove traumatic. You should *never* handle the weight unassisted in your weak range, as it is, by definition, too heavy for that range.

You may also elect to use a power rack, Smith machine, or other device that permits you to rest the weight in the position of your strongest range before you even begin to lift. We prefer this method whenever practical; it is an absolute guarantee that the weight will not descend into your weak range since there are physical barriers that prevent it.

STATIC "REPS"

In the common sense of the term, there are no repetitions performed during the Golfer's Two-Minute Workout. Rather than moving the weight up and down ten to fifteen times as in conventional training, the weight is held motionless in one position. In each of the six exercises, this is done only once per workout. We have determined through other studies that adding a second, third, or more "sets" will not only not improve your results but will hinder them.

WORKOUT ZERO

The first step in starting the Golfer's Two-Minute Workout is to establish your baseline level of strength in terms of static contractions. In many ways this will be the most demanding workout that you perform. You may do all twelve exercises at once or divide them over two or more days. The object of Workout Zero is to discover what level of static strength you possess at the beginning of the program. Most people have never performed static contraction exercises and therefore have no idea what their abilities are. And they always guess too low! For example, the women in this study typically used a leg extension weight of 20 to 40 pounds when training conventionally. So what would you expect them to be able to hold

A POWER RACK POSITIONS THE WEIGHT IN THE PROPER POSITION BEFORE THE EXERCISE AND ENSURES THAT THE WEIGHT CANNOT DESCEND INTO THE WEAK RANGE OF MOTION.

statically? Well, their leg extension for Workout Zero ranged between 90 and 130 pounds!

During the ten seconds that they held that weight we knew they were thinking we might be irresponsible researchers who were dangerously overtaxing their abilities. But the fact is that their old training was of such low intensity and high duration that they had no idea of what they were capable. Three workouts later these women were working with 190 to 210 pounds, and their Workout Zero weights felt like a feather. Imagine how their conventional weights of 20 to 40 pounds felt! The 20-second time limit keeps you honest. When you select a weight that you can only hold for a maximum of 20 seconds, you end up needing more weight than you expect. For example, suppose at the present you perform lat pulldowns with 50 pounds. You might select 75 pounds for a static hold, only to discover that you can hold it statically for over 30 seconds without much fatigue. By going to 100 pounds you find that you can only hold it for 15 seconds. Perfect—now you know your starting weight. Next workout you simply try to hold 100 pounds for 20 seconds. And you will. The fact is that Workout Zero will be more intense than what your muscles are accustomed to, and it will stimulate new muscle strength. Your next workout will see improvement right across the board—it always does.

THE WORKOUT

WORKOUT "A"

Bench Press

Start by lying back on a flat bench. If utilizing a Universal machine bench press, have your partner assist you in lifting the handlebars upward until your arms are fully extended. From this position, bend your elbows slightly so that the resistance is lowered one to two inches and hold this position for 10 to 20 seconds.

If you are using free weights, make sure that you do all of your lifting inside a power rack. Set the pins in the rack to three to

BENCH PRESS HOLD POSITION

four inches below your full lock-out reach. Place your feet flat on the floor for balance. Your grip should be medium width so that, as you lower the bar, your forearms are straight up and down (vertical). Raise the barbell from the pins and lock it out directly above your chest. With the bar directly above your chest, lower the bar until there's a slight bend in your elbows—not such a bend that the barbell touches the pins in the power rack, but enough that it comes close to touching. Hold this position for 10 to 20 seconds.

Lat Pulldowns

To begin, take a close underhand grip on the bar, either kneeling on the floor or on a seat with your knees hooked under the support. Your arms should be stretched fully above your head,

LAT PULLDOWN HOLD POSITION

and you should feel the pull mostly in your lats and somewhat in your biceps. Pull the bar just slightly down—about two to three inches of travel—and hold this position for 10 to 20 seconds. (Note: When your strength exceeds the limit of the weight stack, this movement can be performed unilaterally by attaching a pulley handle to the lat bar attachment and pulling down with one arm for 10 to 20 seconds, and then repeating the procedure with the opposite arm.)

Shoulder Press

This movement can be performed either seated or standing. If performed seated with a Universal machine, place a stool between the handles of the shoulder press station of the machine. Sit on the stool facing toward the weight stack and lock your legs around the uprights of the stool to secure your body in position. If performed standing while utilizing a Universal machine, assume a split stance. Taking an overgrip on the handles attached to the lever arm of the station, have a partner assist you in lifting the handles upward to straight arms-length overhead. Lower the handlebars slightly; hold this position for 10 to 20 seconds.

If performing this exercise with free weights, do so in a power rack or Smith machine. Adjust the height of your support so that the bar is about two inches below the height of a fully extended rep. From a standing position, with your hands approximately three inches wider than your shoulders on each side, press the bar upward until your elbows are locked. Lower the bar slightly, just enough to break the lock in your elbows. Hold for 10 to 20 seconds.

Leg Extension

Sit on a leg-extension machine and place your feet behind the roller pads so that your knees are snug against the seat. Keeping your head and shoulders straight, have your partner assist you

SHOULDER PRESS HOLD POSITION

in raising the roller pad until both legs are straight and your quadriceps are fully contracted. Hold for 10 to 20 seconds. (Note: This movement can also be performed unilaterally by having your partner lift the resistance up into the fully contracted position for you, and then having you support the resistance with only one leg for 10 to 20 seconds. Then repeat with the other leg.)

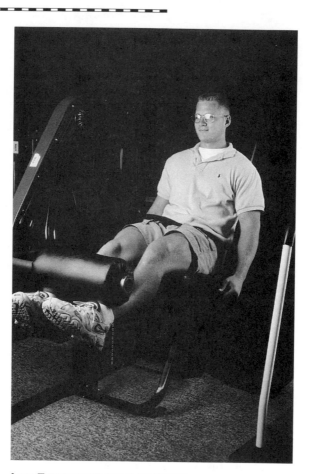

LEG EXTENSION HOLD POSITION

Leg Curl

Lie facedown on the leg-curl machine and place your feet under
the roller pads with your knees just over the edge of the bench.
Have your partner help you lift the roller pads as you slowly curl
your lower legs up until the pads are almost touching your
buttocks. Hold this position for 10 to 20 seconds. (Note: This
movement can also be performed unilaterally; have your partner

LEG CURL HOLD POSITION

raise the roller pad up to the fully contracted position for you,
then utilize only the hamstring strength of one leg—not two—to
sustain the contraction for 10 to 20 seconds. Then switch legs.)

Weighted Crunch

To begin, lie on your back on the floor, with your hands behind
your head and your feet flat on the floor or anchored beneath a
secure object. Take hold of the crunch strap or the curling
handle of a low pulley unit and, while trying to keep your chin
on your chest, slowly curl your trunk upward toward a sitting
position. Make sure you hold onto the strap tightly so that your
abdominals are contracting maximally against the resistance.
You'll find that you can only curl up a third of the range you
would if performing a conventional sit-up. This is fine, because
that is all the range of motion that your abdominals require to

WEIGHTED CRUNCH HOLD POSITION

be stimulated to grow stronger. Once you have ascended to a fully contracted position, hold this position for 10 to 20 seconds.

WORKOUT "B"

Nautilus Lower-Back Machine

In our golfing study we made use of a Nautilus Lower-Back Machine, which provided direct resistance to the lumbar muscles

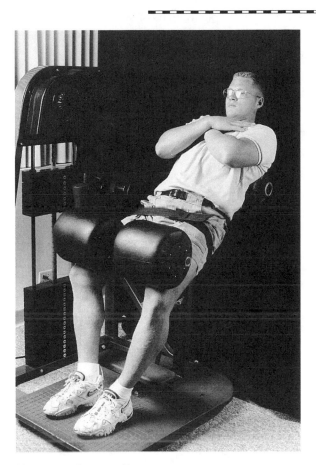

NAUTILUS LOWER-BACK HOLD POSITION

of the lower back. Enter the machine by straddling the seat
bottom. Sit forward in the seat, making sure that your back is
against the highest roller pad. Stabilize your lower body by
moving your thighs under the roller pads and then adjust the
pads until your thighs are securely anchored. Place your feet
firmly on the platform and fasten the seat belt. Placing your hands
across your chest to avoid the temptation of utilizing them to help

"press" you into position, have your partner pull the roller pad backward until your torso is in line with your thighs. Hold this position for 10 to 20 seconds.

Toe Press on a Universal Machine

Sitting down upon the padded seat, brace your back against the upper back pad and adjust the seat position so that your legs, when placed upon the foot pedals, are slightly bent. With the balls of your feet firmly on the foot pedals, slowly press forward until your calves are in a fully contracted position. Hold for 10 to 20 seconds. (Note: This movement can be

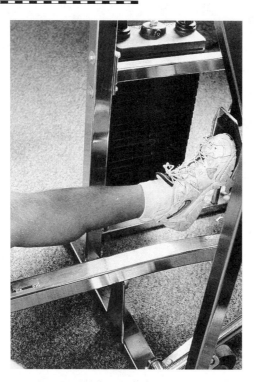

TOE PRESS HOLD POSITION—UNILATERAL

performed unilaterally as well, by simply lifting the resistance
with both legs and then removing one leg from the foot pedal
so that the calf muscle of the remaining leg is bearing the full
resistance. Hold for 10 to 20 seconds per leg.)

Cable Pressdown

Attach a bar handle to the end of the cable running through the
high pulley of a Universal machine (alternatively, you can use a
handle in which the ends are angled downward or one
consisting of two parallel strands of rope). Take an overgrip on

CABLE PRESSDOWN HOLD POSITION

the handle, your index fingers no more than three to four inches apart. Standing erect with your feet about six inches back from the pulley, have your partner help press the bar downward until your arms are perfectly locked out. Bending your elbows slightly so that your triceps—and not your bones—are supporting the resistance, hold for 10 to 20 seconds. (Note: This movement can also be performed unilaterally, by attaching a handle or strap to the lat bar and having your partner assist you into the fully contracted position. Hold for 10 to 20 seconds and then switch arms.)

Cable Curl

Attach a bar handle to the end of the cable running through the floor pulley of a Universal machine. Taking a shoulder-width

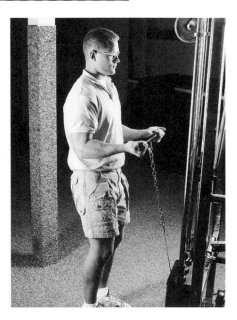

CABLE CURL HOLD POSITION

undergrip on the handle, have your partner assist you in curling the bar up to the halfway position. Hold for 10 to 20 seconds.

Wrist Curl

Take hold of the pulley handle on a Universal machine or a moderately weighted barbell and sit down so that your knees are off the edge of a flat bench. Placing your forearms upon the tops of your thighs with your palms facing upward, have your partner assist you in lifting the resistance up until you've

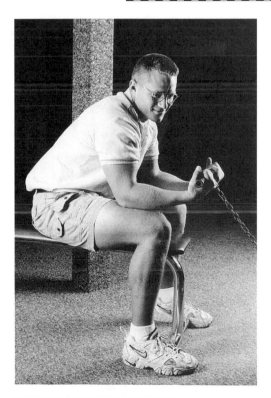

WRIST CURL HOLD POSITION

reached the fully flexed or contracted position for your forearm flexors. Hold for 10 to 20 seconds.

Reverse Wrist Curl

To train the extensor muscles of your forearms, simply reverse the grip on the pulley handle on a Universal machine or a modestly weighted barbell so that your palms are facing downward and have your partner assist you in lifting the bar

REVERSE WRIST CURL HOLD POSITION

upward, so that your knuckles are facing toward the ceiling. Hold for 10 to 20 seconds.

POINTS TO KEEP IN MIND

- **TRAIN WITH A PARTNER OR USE A POWER RACK OR SMITH MACHINE TO LIMIT THE MOVEMENT OF THE WEIGHT.**

- **HOLD THE WEIGHT ONLY BETWEEN 10 AND 20 SECONDS.**

- **USE WEIGHTS THAT ARE HEAVY ENOUGH TO CAUSE TOTAL MUSCULAR FATIGUE WITHIN 10 TO 20 SECONDS.**

- **PERFORM EACH EXERCISE ONLY ONCE PER WORKOUT.**

- **SPACE WORKOUTS FAR ENOUGH APART TO ENSURE PROGRESS IN EVERY WORKOUT.**

- **ONLY COUNT STATIC TIME—DO NOT KEEP THE CLOCK RUNNING WHILE THE WEIGHT DESCENDS.**

ALTERNATE EXERCISES

Lower Back

You may elect to use a free weight deadlift, performed by placing a barbell inside the power rack at a height just slightly above your knees. Stand inside the power rack and grasp the barbell with a grip of approximately shoulder width. Your feet should be under the bar. Slowly pull the barbell upward, making sure to keep your arms straight, until you are fully erect and the barbell is resting on your upper thighs. From this fully erect position, lower the barbell smoothly, bending at the waist approximately three to five inches, while keeping a slight bend in your knees. Hold for 10 to 20 seconds.

You may also perform a seated cable row, using only the muscles of the lower back to raise the resistance. Position your

DEADLIFT HOLD POSITION

SEATED CABLE ROW FOR LOWER BACK, HOLD POSITION

torso on an approximately 45-degree angle and hold it for 10 to 20 seconds.

Forearms

An alternate forearm exercise that stresses the flexor muscles on the underbelly of the forearm is the behind-the-back barbell curl. Hold a barbell (or cable pulley) behind your back at thigh level,

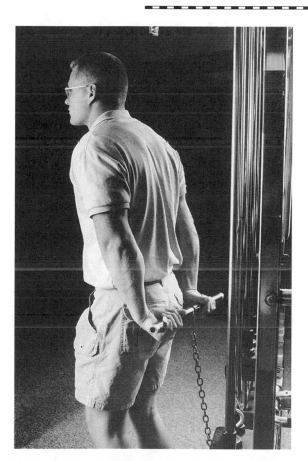

CURL BEHIND BACK CAN BE PERFORMED WITH A BARBELL OR A LOW CABLE PULLEY.

curl the resistance into the fully contracted position, and sustain this for 10 to 20 seconds.

Triceps

A close-grip bench press is an excellent alternate exercise for triceps. It is performed in the same manner as the standard

CLOSE-GRIP BENCH PRESS HOLD POSITION

bench press, except that your hands should be about four inches apart. This places the emphasis on the triceps.

Lats

You may also use a seated low-pulley cable row to overload the lats. From a seated position, lean fully forward and, using only your lat muscles, raise the resistance two to four inches. Hold this position for 10 to 20 seconds.

Legs

An excellent alternate leg exercise is the leg press. A static hold on the leg press provides overload that duplicates the Leg

SEATED CABLE ROW FOR LATS, HOLD POSITION

LEG PRESS HOLD POSITION—UNILATERAL

Curl and Leg Extension at the same time, as it works both the quads and the hamstring muscles. Lock the machine in the highest position, then, without removing the safety locks, press the weight up two to three inches and hold it for 10 to 20 seconds.

Other Exercises

In principle, nearly every exercise can be performed in a strong range static hold. If you decide to do some experimentation, remember to always choose the exercise that permits you to use the most weight for a particular muscle. For example, if you can perform a 10-second hold with 120 pounds in the cable press-down but 200 pounds for 10 seconds in a close-grip bench press, stick with the latter, as it will stimulate more growth.

Chapter 5

THE RESULTS
OF THE STUDY

Armed with the strength increases shown in Chapter 4, we returned to the driving range to remeasure the average driving distance of our eight test subjects. The results were exactly what we and everyone in the study had hoped for. In every case the average distance was increased!

INCREASE IN AVERAGE DRIVE

Just as in the results of the strength training itself, there was a universality of crossover in the subjects. The training resulted

INCREASE IN AVERAGE DRIVE AFTER 14.5 TOTAL MINUTES OF EXERCISE TIME

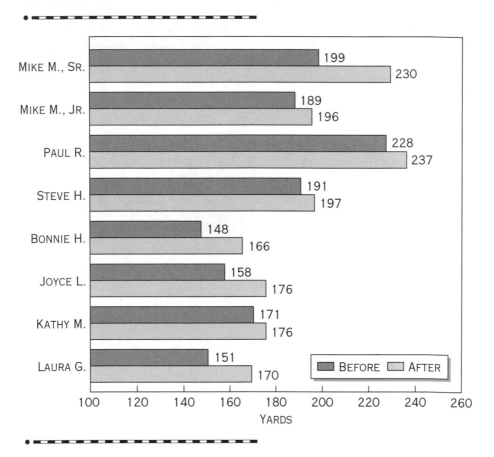

in more strength, and more strength resulted in increased distances on the driving range. As expected, there was considerable variability between individuals. In the case of Mike M., Sr., a relatively modest increase of 60% in overall strength led to an enormous increase in distance of 31 yards. In the case of Steve H., similar strength gains of 56% yielded a smaller increase of 6 yards. The same held true with the women in the study. Kathy M.'s enormous 110% increase in overall strength garnered her a nominal 5-yard increase in her distance, while

INCREASE IN AVERAGE DRIVE AFTER 14.5 TOTAL MINUTES OF EXERCISE TIME

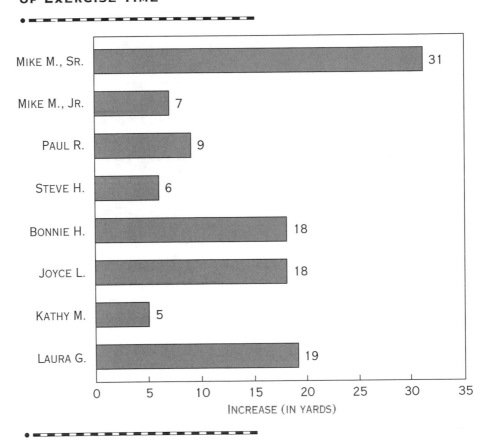

INCREASE (IN YARDS)

Joyce L.'s 73% increase in overall strength yielded her a whopping 18-yard increase in her average drive. These two examples, however, represent the two extremes in the men's and women's group.

COMMENTS FROM THE TEST SUBJECTS

To be sure, everyone was delighted with his or her results in this study. What follows are comments from each of the test subjects. Please note that these comments were made after the final drive measurements were taken but *before* anyone saw the actual data and graphs that showed their true strength or distance increases.

TEST SUBJECT: MIKE M., SR.

"I am definitely hitting the ball a lot farther since doing the workouts— and hitting it farther more consistently. Also, during the time that I was in the study my handicap went from a 14, which I was carrying pretty much all of the year before, to a low this year of 9.7, which put me at 10 over at my club. It was during the time I was doing the study that my handicap improved so dramatically. I thoroughly enjoyed the study. The workouts were tough but not so hard that they weren't enjoyable to look forward to. I felt that I gained quite a bit of strength through the Static Contraction training."

TEST SUBJECT: MIKE M., JR.

"I learned that after lifting weights you need to rest more in order to make progress. I used to lift every day, and when I'd swim I'd really be tired. Now [with Static Contraction training and adequate recovery time] I've learned to slow down on the frequency, as training more frequently doesn't necessarily mean that you will get stronger. I know I've gotten stronger. It was a great training system. I thank Pete and John for doing this and letting me be part of it. I even noticed an improvement in my swimming performances. I'm way stronger and am now clocking some of my best times—with a lot less time spent in the gym."

TEST SUBJECT: PAUL R.

"I feel so much stronger in my golf game. For example, I just played 18 holes this morning and I was hitting really, really well. I hit some great drives. I like the fact that I get the strength without getting bulked up, so that my muscles are able to stay relaxed throughout my swing. My consistency is also much better. When we started the study I know that I was hitting some weaker drives. Now, after six weeks doing the program, my drives are much stronger."

"BEFORE, I WAS ALWAYS WORKING OUT AT THE SAME LEVEL, SO WITH THIS PROGRAM I REALLY FELT THE STRENGTH INCREASE IN LARGE JUMPS."—PAUL R.

"I notice a big increase in my strength. I really do. Even in outside activities. For example, I like to mountain bike and when I'm pedaling up steep inclines, the increase I now have in strength as a result of this program is really noticeable to me. I really notice a huge strength increase

in my legs from this program, and leg strength is very important in the game of golf. I end up using my legs a lot in the swing and with their being stronger now, as a result of the two-minute workouts, it has made a big difference in the power of my swing."

"I see the training method as one that really pushes you to new levels. When I worked out before, I didn't push myself that hard. But because these workouts are so concentrated, you can really push for an increase with each trip to the gym and that, I think, was really the key. It made a huge difference. Before, I was always working out at the same level, so with this program I really felt the strength increase in large jumps."

Note: Paul's nine-yard increase in average drive was measured in the late morning *after* he had just completed playing 18 holes of golf!

TEST SUBJECT: STEVE H.

"In terms of my golf game, I noticed that I now have more strength on difficult lies."

"I find my balance is better and my control has improved. These I attribute directly to the strength I gained from the Golfer's Two-Minute Workout Program."

"During the period that I was in the study I was also trying to push my running up to 40 miles a week. I did that."

"I am definitely stronger—in a major way. I was a little concerned initially about injuries through strength training, but that was never a problem with this program. I think overall you do increase total strength over the course of the study."

"I had a shoulder problem prior to beginning the program. In fact, I thought that it might prove to be a problem in the workout.

However, it didn't seem to be a problem. The training didn't aggravate it at all."

"My endurance has come up a lot since I began the study—now I can't say with certainty that it was solely due to the two-minute workouts, but the role they played in making me stronger certainly has to be considered in the total picture."

TEST SUBJECT: BONNIE H.

"I noticed that I improved tremendously in my short-iron game. I now have a lot of my strength in my short irons. I'm now able to use a pitching wedge from 120 yards, and I'm hitting about 90 to 100 yards with my sand wedge."

"This has really improved my power—even in my fairway irons. I feel more solid and more connected when I hit the ball."

"I notice in my golf game that in stroking the ball, it has become effortless. I feel like I'm now getting a lot of momentum through the ball without having to think about it. I felt strong when I swung my club and, after 18 holes, I always have energy to spare, like I could have gone out and played another nine."

"I personally feel stronger — and that's the truth. I think there's a lot to be said for the concept of holding weights, as opposed to moving them, for the purpose of building strength. I think it is a very rewarding way to train. I have personally been working out with weights for at least 20 years, pretty religiously. I have been pretty athletic all my life, so I was interested in the theory or concept behind the Golfer's Two-Minute Workout: holding weights at a heavier weight than what I would normally use dynamically. I thought it was fascinating. I used to do isometrics for my legs in order to get in shape for skiing, but never got as strong as quickly as I did in this six-week study."

"I've noticed a lot of shape and fitness benefits as well. I have way more energy since starting this program."

"THIS HAS REALLY IMPROVED MY POWER—EVEN IN MY FAIRWAY IRONS. I FEEL MORE SOLID AND MORE CONNECTED WHEN I HIT THE BALL."
—BONNIE H.

"This is something that a lot more people should know about if they want to improve their golf game."

"A lot of women are apprehensive about lifting weights but, believe me, this program will really improve your game."

TEST SUBJECT: JOYCE L.

"I'm hitting the ball much farther now as a result of the strength I got from this program, and I'm also hitting it farther with much greater consistency."

"I've developed strength that I didn't think I had, and this has created a feeling of increased confidence for me. I'm really happy with

"I'VE DEVELOPED STRENGTH THAT I DIDN'T THINK I HAD, AND THIS HAS CREATED A FEELING OF INCREASED CONFIDENCE FOR ME."—JOYCE L.

the increased strength I got. When you don't push yourself in everyday life, and then you do, it's amazing what you are capable of. I find that my energy levels are up. Even though I always walk, I feel like I've got energy."

"I know that my muscles felt more tired after these workouts, even in walking to the car. I like that feeling, because it lets you know that you've really done something productive for the body and that you're going to get some results."

"I enjoyed the program and I would like to do it longer."

TEST SUBJECT: KATHY M.

"Well, I'm superenthusiastic about this program. I believe in weight training, and I found it to be very beneficial. I noticed the improvement the most in my general health and strength. My golf game became far more consistent and just stronger overall. I can now lift the rear gate down on my Ford Explorer with absolutely no difficulty at all. Whenever I came back from shopping, I would always feel a strain in my elbow whenever I would go to close the gate. In fact, if I had a bag of groceries in one hand, I could never close the gate on the Explorer. Now it's no problem at all."

"I'm golfing much better. I played in a tournament recently and am hitting the ball really far now."

"I've also noticed that my body has firmed up; my waist measurement has gone down, and my arms—particularly when I'm blow-drying my hair—my triceps are firm now! There's no hanging, sagging skin there. I really did notice a change in the firmness in my body."

"I love the fact that this program is so lifestyle-friendly. I have time commitments, as most men and women do, and so to have a program that is this effective that only takes two minutes a week to perform is a godsend. This is optimum!"

"I HAVE TIME COMMITMENTS, AS MOST MEN AND WOMEN DO, AND SO TO HAVE A PROGRAM THAT IS THIS EFFECTIVE THAT ONLY TAKES TWO MINUTES A WEEK TO PERFORM IS A GODSEND. THIS IS OPTIMUM!"—KATHY M.

TEST SUBJECT: LAURA G.

"My drives, particularly my 5-wood off the fairway, improved tremendously as a result of this program. I was more balanced, and it didn't seem to take near the effort for me to really hit that ball properly and to hit it a lot farther. It just seemed to happen easier for me after using this program."

"I won a long ball championship recently, hitting the ball farther than all of the other women who participated in the tournament. There were 18 competitors."

"MY DRIVES, PARTICULARLY MY 5-WOOD OFF THE FAIRWAY, IMPROVED TREMENDOUSLY AS A RESULT OF THIS PROGRAM."—LAURA G.

"This was my first weight-training experience and I had never done any type of exercise program prior to this, apart from just walking around the golf course a lot of times. I think I may even have been a little nervous initially, thinking of how hard I was pushing those weights. That was my only concern because I didn't feel that I was in really good shape to begin with."

"My energy [was] way up—even after as little time as my first two workouts. I noticed an energy boost right away."

"I think everybody ought to try this program. And the fact that it helped me tremendously proves that you don't have to be an advanced athlete, or in really good shape, to pick up on the program and get really good results."

SOME MYTHS EXPLODED

To see these results using any form of strength training would be very significant. To see them with a program that uses 1–2% of conventional training time is truly revolutionary. Along with these revelations, we learned that many of the prevailing notions regarding strength training and golf are nothing more than unsubstantiated myths; namely:

"Strength isn't important to a golfer."   Virtually every golfer we spoke to when beginning this study informed us of his or her opinion that strength was not an important component in a powerful golf swing. Our own literary agent, an avid golfer, told us that strength is "a slice of a slice of the total pie." To be sure, a great deal has been written on the importance of swing technique and on the importance of the mental aspects of performance. We are not debating the significance of these elements, but we believe that the paradigm needs to be adjusted to reflect the reality of muscle power in the generation of club-head speed and ball velocity. It is doubtful that golfers at this level could merely adjust their grip or mental focus and see a 20- or 30-yard increase in their average drive, along with a boost in overall energy and physical power. Moreover, the subjects in this study also reported improvements in their short-iron game, their stamina, their balance, and their confidence. The fact is that strength has equal importance with any other single factor in golfing and more importance than many trivial issues that get more attention.

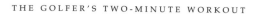

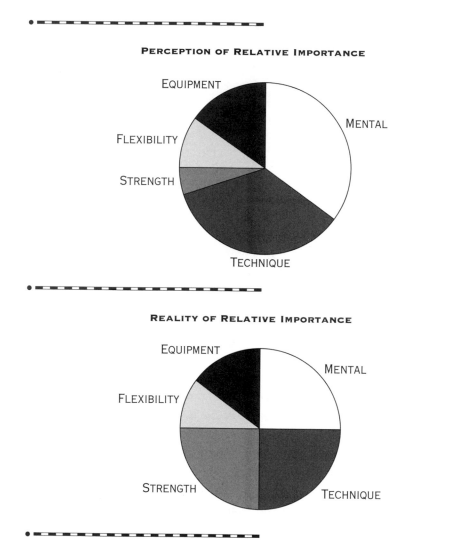

PERCEPTION OF RELATIVE IMPORTANCE

EQUIPMENT

MENTAL

FLEXIBILITY

STRENGTH

TECHNIQUE

REALITY OF RELATIVE IMPORTANCE

EQUIPMENT

MENTAL

FLEXIBILITY

STRENGTH

TECHNIQUE

The top graph above represents the typical perception of the "whole pie" as viewed by most golfers.

The bottom graph above represents a more accurate depiction of reality, particularly as it relates to factors that affect maximum driving distance, power, and energy levels.

"To gain strength you have to hit the gym three days a week."
Another myth, which incidentally permeates every sport, is that
strength increases are hard won and only garnered from long,
brutal, three-day-a-week workouts of an hour or more. This
myth is sometimes further augmented by the belief that enormous quantities of food, particularly protein, must be
consumed in order for any strength gains to manifest. The
reality is that the subjects on this study, who were all middle-
aged but one, achieved very substantial increases in strength
with a comparatively trifling amount of exercise. Furthermore,
we asked them to make no changes in their diet, golfing, exercise, or other normal routine. These subjects nearly doubled
their strength by averaging one two-minute workout per week
over just six weeks.

"Maintaining your strength requires frequent workouts."   It is also
widely believed that strength training is identical to aerobic
conditioning, which must be performed three to five times per
week to prevent the benefits from quickly fading. We have
compiled considerable data to prove that this is not the case. In
this study we need look no further than Joyce L. and Laura G.,
who had 24 days elapse between their last workout and the
final measurement of their drive distances. The 24 days not only
consisted of no workouts, but also involved two transatlantic
airplane flights and a week of holidays, which, as we all know,
usually leads to overindulgence rather than our usual discipline
of eating and exercise. Despite this, Joyce and Laura both
demonstrated enormous increases in their performance. We
have many similar cases from other studies that involve total
layoffs of six, eight, and more weeks without any deterioration
of strength and power. The fact is that for these very test
subjects we would recommend a modified training schedule of
one workout every ten days to two weeks, with an eye toward
extending that frequency to one workout every three or four
weeks as a means to maintain a level of strength with which
they are comfortable. We further believe, and expect future

studies to corroborate, that enlightened strength-training regimens of the future will involve workouts of one minute or less of exercise, performed with about the same frequency with which you get a haircut.

Don't let mythology affect your thinking when it comes to strength training to improve your golf game. This study clearly and unambiguously shows that enormous increases in strength and power are achievable with very brief but very intense exercises. Furthermore, these workouts can be spaced very far apart without fear of muscular atrophy or loss of strength. There is also no need to risk injuries to muscles, tendons, and ligaments by handling heavy weights through a full range of motion. Merely supporting heavy weights in the safest, strongest range position will ensure substantial muscle growth stimulation.

We know that using the word "revolutionary" can sound a little self-serving on our part, but when a means of obtaining increased strength and distance for golfers is achieved with a nearly 99% reduction in time compared to conventional methods, what other word can we use? What would you think if your morning commute to work could be reduced from thirty minutes to thirty seconds, or if it took you two and a half months to go from mailroom clerk to CEO, instead of twenty years! In this world, 99% reductions in time in any field of endeavor are very rare, so rare as to be truly revolutionary.

Chapter 6

PROGRESS AND

OVERTRAINING

OVERTRAINING

If you follow the guidelines of this program to the letter, you
will experience an absolute minimum of overtraining. We
cannot say "zero" overtraining, because the frequency of workouts actually remains fixed until the first sign of overtraining.
For example, you might train once per week for nine weeks
with steady progress but on the tenth week notice that your
numbers did not improve. That, in the simplest terms, means
that you just engaged in overtraining. This will be immediately
apparent when you record your numbers in your Workout Log.

When this occurs you simply need to space your workouts further apart.

If you stubbornly continue to train on a too-frequent basis you will develop a number of telltale symptoms. The most common are an almost constant sense of fatigue, combined with a deep lack of energy and ambition. Other signs include:

- **FREQUENT COLDS AND INJURIES**

- **PERSISTENT SORENESS AND STIFFNESS IN THE MUSCLES, JOINTS, OR TENDONS**

- **HEAVYLEGGEDNESS**

- **LOSS OF INTEREST IN TRAINING**

- **INABILITY TO RELAX**

- **A DECREASE IN ACADEMIC WORK OR PERFORMANCE**

- **SLEEP PROBLEMS**

- **HEADACHES**

- **LOSS OF APPETITE**

One of the more popular methods used to detect overtraining is to monitor the morning pulse rate. Upon arising, the athlete is instructed to take his pulse for 60 seconds. If it is seven beats a minute faster than usual, a layoff or reduction in training is recommended. Perhaps the most blatant symptom of overtraining is a very strong disinclination to train at all, as your body is signaling your brain that it hasn't fully recovered from the cumulative systemic toll of previous training sessions. Any person who falls into the habit of training five and six days a week over prolonged periods of time will inevitably become overtrained, regardless of how powerful or well built an individual may be.

THE NECESSITY OF A TRAINING LOG BOOK

As there are many exercises, weights, and hold times to be remembered in the Golfer's Two-Minute Workout, it's exceedingly difficult to mentally retain all of the knowledge that you have gathered. Steady progress can only be ensured by using a proper log to record the specifics of each workout.

These Workout Log forms may be photocopied for your own use. You will notice that Workout As are numbered 1, 3, 5, 7, etc., and Workout Bs are numbered 2, 4, 6, 8, etc., to ensure that they are done alternately. When you complete Workouts 11 and

THE GOLFER'S TWO-MINUTE WORKOUT LOG

	ZERO	ONE	THREE	FIVE	SEVEN	NINE	ELEVEN
				WORKOUT A			
EXERCISE	DATE: 4/7/98	DATE: 4/21/98	DATE: 5/7/98	DATE: 5/21/98	DATE: 6/7/98	DATE:	DATE:
BENCH PRESS	190 lbs. / 12 sec.	190 / 20	210 / 11	210 / 19	225 / 16	/	/
LAT PULLDOWN	50 lbs. / 14 sec.	50 / 21	60 / 18	70 / 10	70 / 20	/	/
SHOULDER PRESS	90 lbs. / 10 sec.	90 / 16	100 / 12	100 / 22	110 / 14	/	/
LEG EXTENSION	80 lbs. / 13 sec.	80 / 20	95 / 10	95 / 20	100 / 16	/	/
LEG CURL	60 lbs. / 19 sec.	75 / 14	80 / 20	85 / 12	85 / 18	/	/
WEIGHTED CRUNCH	20 lbs. / 10 sec.	20 / 20	30 / 10	30 / 18	35 / 12	/	/

THE GOLFER'S TWO-MINUTE WORKOUT LOG

	ZERO	ONE	THREE	FIVE	SEVEN	NINE	ELEVEN
EXERCISE	DATE:	DATE:	DATE:	DATE:	DATE:	DATE:	DATE:
BENCH PRESS	/	/	/	/	/	/	/
LAT PULLDOWN	/	/	/	/	/	/	/
SHOULDER PRESS	/	/	/	/	/	/	/
LEG EXTENSION	/	/	/	/	/	/	/
LEG CURL	/	/	/	/	/	/	/
WEIGHTED CRUNCH	/	/	/	/	/	/	/

THE GOLFER'S TWO-MINUTE WORKOUT LOG

	ZERO	TWO	FOUR	SIX	EIGHT	TEN	TWELVE
EXERCISE	DATE:	DATE:	DATE:	DATE:	DATE:	DATE:	DATE:
NAUTILUS LOW-BACK	/	/	/	/	/	/	/
TOE PRESS	/	/	/	/	/	/	/
CABLE PRESSDOWN	/	/	/	/	/	/	/
CABLE CURL	/	/	/	/	/	/	/
WRIST CURL	/	/	/	/	/	/	/
REVERSE WRIST CURL	/	/	/	/	/	/	/

12, enter those numbers under Workout Zero on fresh A and B pages of the Workout Logs and continue training. We cannot overstate the importance of using these in the success of this program. Please make certain you use them.

On page 87 is an example of how the Workout Log is used. Please notice how the weights and times show progression from workout to workout.

Chapter 7

THE
THEORETICAL
PRINCIPLES

The Golfer's Two-Minute Workout is a method of training that focuses on static contractions—the taxing of each individual muscle group in the one position that will engage the maximum amount of muscle fibers. Further, the muscle should be stressed in this position over a 10- to 20-second time span.

When using the Golfer's Two-Minute Workout you must throw out all preconceived notions of training methodology. You will no longer be using repetitions by which to gauge your progress;

from now on you will be counting seconds. You will no longer be looking for a variety of exercises to tax the various aspects of a muscle; instead you will use only one exercise per body part. That one exercise, however, will of necessity call into play all of the targeted muscle group's various muscle fibers and stimulate them over the period of time you will be maximally contracting, up until each fiber has been individually and thoroughly taxed and you can no longer continue to hold the resistance statically.

THE THEORY

The Golfer's Two-Minute Workout is a logical system and consequently can be successfully grasped by anyone if they comprehend the basic tenets behind it. The fact that most of the material contained herein is based upon empirically validated data, going back over 120 years in some instances, as well as common sense (as opposed to commercial interests), means that what has worked in the physiology labs can be repeated with equal, if not better, success. We guarantee that if you do this, you will make progress in your game during the span of one month, which would have otherwise taken you many months or even several years to achieve.

It is essential when embarking upon a system such as the Golfer's Two-Minute Workout to understand some of the basic physiological principles, such as the law of muscle fiber recruitment and the "all or none" principle of muscle fiber contraction, in order to reap the full benefits of this training method.

ALL OR NONE

With regard to the "all or none" principle of exercise physiology, it states in effect that when a muscle contracts, the smallest percentage of its available fibers as are required to generate the required force to sustain or move the resistance will contract maximally—for all they're worth—while the rest of the fibers within that muscle will not contract at all. This is opposed to the common belief that all of a working muscle's fibers contract at once but to a lesser degree.

In other words, an individual muscle fiber will contract maximally or not at all. This is a bipolar condition peculiar to muscle tissue and is immutable. With this in mind, it stands to reason that the surest way to involve the most muscle fibers possible in a given contraction is to engage the muscle group you are training in the one position in its range of motion in which all its fibers can be activated—and then sustaining this position of maximum fiber involvement (thereby firing off as many fibers as possible) for as long as possible.

THE PROBLEM WITH REPETITIONS

In conventional training methods, a typical set sees one start a given movement in a position of literally "zero" resistance. Then, as the weight is moved, the muscle shortens, or contracts, into a position of slightly greater tension until it finally ascends to a position of full or maximal contraction. And it is this final position in which the most stress (the stimulus that induces a muscle to grow stronger) is applied to the muscle and, as a result, the one position throughout the muscle's range of move-ment that involves the most muscle fibers. The problem lies in the fact that this position of maximal contraction and fiber involvement is, at least in traditional training methods, over almost before it begins.

For example, take one of the easiest exercises around: the leg extension. You place your legs under the pads of a leg-extension machine, lift your legs up until you contract your quadriceps (to full extension), and slowly return to the starting position. Now, at the beginning of the movement you're using only the barest number of muscle fibers. At the halfway point, a few more muscle fibers get called into play. Then, at the position of full muscular contraction, you've finally done what you set out to do; you're actually forcing a large number of your muscle fibers to get in on the act. However, what typically happens at this point is that long before the fibers can be stressed maximally, the resistance is lowered (often dropped) just as you reach the point of full contraction, and long before the fibers have had time to be fully stressed, giving the momentarily stressed quadriceps muscles a chance to disengage and recover.

What this means, in effect, is that in a given ten-rep set performed in the conventional manner as just described, you have a set that, from first rep to last, takes roughly ten seconds to perform. Now in that ten-second time frame, the quadriceps muscles of your upper thighs have been placed in a position of maximum contraction for approximately ten percent of the time it took you to complete the set, or *one* second. In other words, out of a possible ten seconds' worth of maximum muscular involvement, which, let us not forget, parlays into direct strength stimulation, the trainee is obtaining only one-tenth of the results that he/she is capable of generating from the movement. The reality of the situation is that they're wasting the other nine-tenths of the time they employ on the exercise.

Conversely, when a given muscle group is made to contract maximally against resistance, all of its muscle fibers that can be activated to assist with the task will be activated and subsequently fatigued. It is this methodology that makes this system so effective, and which separates it from all other training systems.

STATIC CONTRACTION VS. ISOMETRICS

Some people may say, "Oh, I get it—you're contracting your muscles against an immovable object—that's isometrics!"

A POWERFUL GOLF SWING INVOLVES MUSCLES OF THE LEGS, ABDOMINALS, ARMS, CHEST, SHOULDERS, AND BACK.

Wrong. This definition does not fit. The Golfer's Two-Minute Workout features the technique of Static Contraction training, wherein your muscles are pitted not against an immovable object—as is the case with isometrics—but rather against a level of resistance that can be measured, quantified, and varied almost infinitely. Plus, the resistance has to be moved into a position of full muscular contraction before the set can be initiated.

In addition, isometrics only initiates contraction in the position where the fewest number of muscle fibers are activated, that is, at the beginning of most movements, such as the bottom quarter of the military press or the bottom quarter of a "door-knob curl," etc. The inherent problem with isometrics is that it never allows the muscle you're training to progress beyond this minimal level of fiber involvement.

The Golfer's Two-Minute Workout utilizes complete and absolute muscular contraction with resistance, which allows far greater strength-inducing methods to be employed. With golfers, for example, we've found that very heavy compound movements work best (as opposed to isolation exercises), as they serve to increase the intensity level of the workouts tremendously. In fact, this type of training is so demanding that most of our golfers require a minimum of perhaps one week's rest to allow for full muscular and systemic recovery to take place and growth to occur before they can perform their next workout.

WHY STATIC CONTRACTION TRAINING IS SO EFFECTIVE

The reason for the dramatic success of the Golfer's Two-Minute Workout lies in the very nature of Static Contraction. Any time movement is involved in exercise, you're simply doing one thing—moving your muscles out of a position of full contraction—that is a step in the wrong direction.

Full muscular contraction is the only position in any muscle's range of motion in which maximum fiber stimulation can take place. Therefore, anything involving either positive (+) or negative (–) movement, either toward or away from this one position has, perforce, varying levels of intensity. As has been mentioned, the closer your muscles are to a position of full muscular contraction (wherein the maximal resistance is held in a position of full muscular contraction), the greater the intensity generated and the more muscle fibers you will have activated. The more fibers you stimulate, the more they grow as a result of having been stimulated. If you're not in a position of full muscular contraction, you're not involving as many muscle fibers as you could be and consequently you're not stimulating the maximum number of muscle fibers available. As a result, you're not stimulating the muscle maximally.

Chapter 8

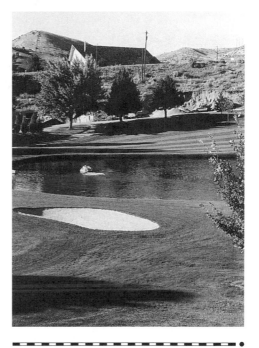

MUSCLES—
YOUR "GOLFING
MACHINE"

We hope that you are now beginning to appreciate the "physical game of golf." After all, it is the principles of physics that determine the motion of the ball, and it is the physiology of your muscles that creates the energy and force necessary for you to swing your club. While there can be no downplaying of the significance of technique in becoming a better golfer, it should also be remembered that all the technique in the world is useless—if you lack the strength necessary to execute it. Furthermore, as good as your technique is, if you were stronger you would be able to hit the ball harder.

To this end, it behooves the serious student of the game of golf to first get to know the principal player—him or herself. Not yourself in terms of what your name, age, and social security number is, but the inner workings of the golfing machine that is your body. Within your body there exists three distinct classes or types of muscle.

One class is cardiac muscle, which is responsible for the contractions of your heart, which are not unlike the contractions of any one of the six hundred discernible skeletal muscles throughout the body. One of the microscopic differences that separates cardiac muscle from skeletal muscle is the existence of a form of physiological "generator" on certain cardiac muscle cells called "pacemaker cells." What these do is send out signals to the heart that stimulate it to contract. As their name implies, the function of these cells has given rise to the concept of the pacemaker, the device worn by victims of heart disease.

The second general class of muscle is known either as "smooth" or "visceral" and is found lining the walls of the internal organs (i.e., the viscera). These muscles assist in the transportation of food and waste materials to their proper destinations.

The third class of muscle, and the one that most golfers should be concerned with, is skeletal muscle. These, of course, are the muscles of the body that are responsible for all of the many movements we engage in on a daily basis. Skeletal muscles are attached from one bone to another across one or more joints. Their shortening, or contraction, allows us to move.

CONTRACTION

Skeletal muscle has only one function: to shorten or contract. This being the case, it immediately becomes apparent that training directives that tell you to "pull the club" or "push the putt" are malapropisms of the highest order. The function of skeletal muscle has nothing to do with either of these two things. The proteins, the molecular components that make up muscle fiber, cannot "push" outward any more than a moose can fly—it's simply not in a fiber's physiological makeup. And yet, having said this, it would appear, if only superficially, that we can "push" things away from us by using our muscles. After all, we perform "push-ups" and "push open" doors. If the term doesn't exist in the realm of physiology, it's certainly alive and well in the world of our popular vocabulary.

But what actually happens when we "push" something? Simply the activation of an antagonistic group of muscle fibers. All muscles are paired on opposite sides of a bone or a limb. There is no anatomical exception to this rule; all muscles appear in pairs (the "every action has an equal and opposite reaction" law of Newtonian physics). For example, your quadriceps are paired with your hamstrings, your forearm flexors are paired with your extensors, and your biceps are opposite your triceps. Here's how it works: Let us suppose you've just "pushed" the resistance upward on a leg-press machine from your chest to the fully extended position of the movement. Your hamstrings, or "leg biceps," are located on the lower surface of your femur, or "thigh bone," and attach to your lower leg. When they contract, they bring your heel and lower leg closer to your buttocks. Your quadriceps, located on the top surface of your femur, are also attached to your lower leg and are stretched whenever the hamstrings are contracted. Now, if you want to "push" that weight back to the starting position, you engage or contract your quadriceps muscle, which in turn extends the lower leg back to the starting position while at the same time stretching your hamstring muscles (again, the "every action has an equal and opposite reaction" law). All in all, you get the appearance of "pushing" through the actual drawing together of muscle tissue.

THE BIG PICTURE

As we've now pointed out (in a very general way) how certain muscle groups function, it should be noted that these muscle groups usually comprise anywhere from two to four muscles— a form of "team effort," if you will, at least as far as movement is involved. Some muscles arise from one bone in two or three different places, only to join or insert into a second bone as one muscle. Now hold on, there's nothing mystical or theological

about this; it's not a "wonders of the Holy Trinity" type of thing, just human physiology in action, pure and simple. Here's a sampling of some of these "team" muscles:

HAMSTRINGS: THIS MUSCLE GROUP IS COMPOSED OF THREE MUSCLES: THE SEMITENDINOSUS, THE SEMIMEMBRANOSUS AND THE BICEPS FEMORIS, WHICH ARE SITUATED BEHIND THE FEMUR, OR THIGH BONE.

QUADRICEPS: THIS IS A FOUR-MUSCLE COMPOSITE CONSISTING OF THE VASTUS LATERALIS, THE VASTUS MEDIALIS, THE VASTUS INTERMEDIUS, AND THE RECTUS FEMORIS. ALL THESE MUSCLES RESIDE ON THE FRONT OF THE FEMUR.

DELTOIDS: THIS IS A THREE-MUSCLE TEAM THAT COVERS THE ENTIRE SHOULDER CAP. IT CONSISTS OF THE ANTERIOR DELTOID (THE FRONT HEAD), THE LATERAL DELTOID (THE SIDE HEAD), AND THE POSTERIOR DELTOID (THE REAR HEAD). EACH HEAD OF THE DELTOID POSSESSES AN INDIVIDUAL FUNCTION THAT RESULTS IN SHOULDER MOVEMENT, AND SPECIFIC EXERCISES ARE REQUIRED TO FULLY STIMULATE EACH HEAD OF THE MUSCLE.

BICEPS: A TWO-HEADED MUSCLE THAT ORIGINATES ON TWO POINTS OF THE SCAPULA AND INSERTS INTO ONE POINT IN THE FOREARM.

TRICEPS: A THREE-HEADED MUSCLE WITH THREE DIFFERENT ORIGINS ON THE SHOULDER, WHICH COME TOGETHER TO INSERT INTO ONE ATTACHMENT ON THE FOREARM. DIFFERENT EXERCISES WILL STRESS (TO A LIMITED DEGREE) DIFFERENT HEADS OF THE MUSCLE.

THE SMALLER PICTURE

Each muscle is composed of fibers that, collectively, form specific muscles. Each muscle fiber, as small as it is, is nevertheless the shell of a bundle of even smaller fibers. These smaller fibers are known as "myofibrils," and even these contain smaller fibrous components known as "myofilaments."

So, to repeat, you've got muscles that are made up of bundles of fibers, which are made up of bundles of myofibrils, which, in turn, are made up of bundles of myofilaments. Here's a staggering statistic from the world of science: the average person has been estimated to have over one quarter of a billion muscle fibers in his body. You can well appreciate the math

FROM WALKING ACROSS THE ROOM TO CONTEMPLATING THE LIE OF THE GREEN, ATP IS THE ENERGY THAT'S RUNNING THE SHOW.

required to calculate the total amount of myofilaments one might have! In any event, what all of these bundles have in common, from the fiber down to the myofilament, is the function of contraction. To this end, they enlist the aid of two of the four proteins that reside in muscle tissue—*actin* and *myosin*. Both actin and myosin are referred to as "contractile proteins" because their function is to hook up and shorten or contract, which creates muscular force or "tension," which in turn, as we learned in Chapter 3, is so important for stimulating muscle growth. The remaining two proteins are *troponin* and *tropomyosin*, and their role is likened to that of an "off switch" mechanism for the actin and myosin.

The nature of actin and myosin is that, when left unimpeded, they seek out each other and draw toward one another. Unless the other two proteins, i.e., the troponin and tropomyosin, step into the equation, actin and myosin find each other, with the result that muscular contraction occurs. In fact, were it not for the "wedgelike" effect of troponin and tropomyosin, you would be in constant agony (cramping) because your muscles would always be contracted maximally.

Having stated that proteins are a part of muscle tissue, I should point out that protein isn't the whole of muscle tissue. Furthermore, it doesn't follow that you require a lot of supplemental protein (such as pills or powders) in your diet in order to build stronger muscles for golf. The truth of the matter is that only 22% of a muscle is composed of protein; the remainder of the muscle, more than 70% of its composition, is water. You will do nothing to hasten the muscle growth process by consuming excessive amounts of protein.

THE ROOT OF CONTRACTION

Muscle contraction begins with an electrical signal from the central nervous system. When the current arrives at the muscle it is immediately transferred up and down the length and depth of the muscle through a relay system of tubules. When the message reaches each one of the thousands of receptor sites, it drops off a little shot of calcium. What calcium does is bring about a blocking or "inhibitory" effect on the noncontractile proteins (troponin and tropomyosin), which—up until the calcium showed up—had been doing their job of keeping the actin and myosin proteins separated.

The calcium, however, has the same effect on troponin and tropomyosin that Kryptonite has on Superman; it takes away their power to perform, i.e., to separate actin and myosin, by inhibiting their ability to function—and their function, of course, is to keep the "contractile" proteins from contracting. Further analysis reveals this process even more clearly when we look at what's called a *sarcomere*, which is simply one individual unit of actin and myosin. At each end of the sarcomere is a rather broad anchoring structure called a "Z-disc." And extending inward from each Z-disc are thin strands of actin protein, which just manage to overlap the much thicker strands of myosin protein that reside smack dab in the middle of each sarcomere.

The interesting thing about myosin protein strands are that they have little receptor sites that emanate outward from either side of their main body that, schematically, resemble something of a cross between little hooks and the strands of a feather. Technically, these receptor sites are called "cross-bridges," as they serve to "bridge," or connect, the actin and myosin contractile proteins. Once the electrical charge for contraction arrives via the nerve cells from the brain to the muscle, they drop off a little packet of calcium, which immediately severs the leashlike effect of the troponin and tropomyosin. With the "leash" removed, so to speak, several rather phenomenal occurrences take place involving the now free-floating actin and myosin: The cross-bridges rotate and by so doing draw inward on the actin filaments and Z-discs ever so slightly. The cross-bridges begin to attach to the actin protein strands. The proteins themselves undergo a change in shape. The sarcomere shortens as both Z-discs are drawn inward.

When many of these sarcomeres shorten simultaneously, the muscle fibers and then the muscle itself contract. And, although some textbooks may tell you that the shortening of the sarcomere is caused by the release of energy caused by a break-down of ATP (adenosine triphosphate), this is not the case. In fact, the process of contraction will occur automatically when-ever calcium enters the picture and inhibits the restrictive func-tion of the troponin and tropomyosin proteins. ATP is present and required, however, for the cross-bridges to release and return to their "resting" position until they're required to contract again. An example of this can be seen if you flex the biceps muscle in your upper arm; this is the result of thousands of contractions and (if you extend your forearm) releases by the cross-bridges, with the contracting portion precipitated by the presence of calcium and the releases fueled by the energy gener-ated by the breakdown of ATP.

THE ROLE OF ATP

All right then, what's this ATP? Quite simply, ATP is the rock-bottom, brass-tacks, bedrock, grassroots fuel for all bodily func-tions. From walking across the room to contemplating the lie of the green, ATP is the energy that's running the show. ATP has been described as a miniature warehouse of energy—and it is. ATP is made up of three phosphate groups: oxygen, phos-phorus, and adenosine. The adenosine is really a molecule to which the oxygen and phosphorus bond to form the chemical compound adenosine triphosphaste (ATP).

When energy is required for a powerful swing of a driver, ATP is the first one out of the blocks to provide it—usually by breaking off one of the phosphate groups, which leaves *adenosine diphosphate,* or ADP. The result of this is that a good portion of energy is released for immediate use by the muscles (ADP cannot be broken down further into AMP, or adenosine monophosphate, by the muscles themselves, but, if needed, this can occur elsewhere in the body to create more energy for movement).

Let us suppose you are about to begin the Golfer's Two-Minute Workout and, having just come off a seven-day layoff, your energy reserves and ATP stores are completely replenished. At the start of your exercise session, you have roughly three ounces of ATP in your entire body to expend for energy. This will be adequate to keep any muscle contracting for roughly three seconds. If your set is going to last longer than three seconds (which of course it will), you're going to need more ATP energy to successfully complete the duration of your set. So where's it going to come from? Well, the energy transporter in this case is another chemical compound, called CP, or creatine phosphate.

When CP is broken down into its molecular components of creatine and phosphate, the energy that is thus released can hook up with an ADP molecule and attach to it a loose phosphate molecule to create a new ATP molecule. And, the neat part is that there's enough CP stored in your body to keep up this ATP conversion process for a solid ten seconds.

THE ANAEROBIC PATHWAYS

There exist but two types of training pathways as mapped out by your central nervous system—the anaerobic and aerobic. However, for the purposes of building stronger muscles you want to remain exclusively in the anaerobic pathways. Aerobic activity, as the name implies, burns mainly body fat for fuel and requires the presence of oxygen to do so. Aerobic training is a necessity if your objective is endurance-related activities, such as distance running, cross-country skiing, or other such activities where endurance is a factor. However, as your objective is stimulating muscle growth and strength, you want to burn solely glycogen as your fuel of choice, which is stored within the muscles you are training.

The first 10 to 60 seconds of contraction of a given muscle are fueled by energy that is largely derived from your anaerobic system. The reason you want to wrap things up in under 20 seconds in Static Contraction training is that, for the purposes of generating substantial increases in strength, the weight you are contracting against is more important than the amount of time, or duration, that you are contracting against it. Besides, if your set lasts too long, as many conventional exercise protocols advocate, at about the two-minute mark in training, your system will start to employ the use of the aerobic pathways to help with the workload. In fact, after 90 to 100 seconds, the aerobic system is responsible for 50% of your energy output, which means, in effect, that you're splitting your training stimulus for muscle mass in half—with the new request for more aerobic (i.e., the system that employs oxygen to burn off proteins, carbs, and fats for fuel) assistance utilizing 50% of the stimulus that could have been geared solely for muscle growth.

THE IMPORTANCE OF CARBOHYDRATES

It follows from this that carbohydrates, the primary fuel of muscles operating within the anaerobic pathways (since carbohydrates are the ones most readily converted to glycogen) are the nutrient of choice for the serious golfer looking to increase his strength through a productive Static Contraction workout.

Carbohydrates are the sole fuel for training anaerobically, which is what you want to do to stimulate increases in strength. It takes the body up to 50 minutes of continuous exercise to begin the breakdown of fats for energy and, if carbohydrate stores are low in the body, your system will turn first to protein—which is most readily available from your lean body tissue (i.e., your muscles).

What this means is that if adequate carbohydrate isn't available for the contracting muscles through the foods you eat, the body will consume your existing stores of muscle mass for fuel! Another interesting side note for those who habitually engage in low-carbohydrate diets for the purpose of shedding body fat is that they lose out on a small compound that forms as a result of the breakdown of carbohydrate into the bloodstream. This compound, glucose, is one that is essential for the metabolism of fat within the body. All this is quite apart from the fact that the human brain derives 99.9% of the nutrition it needs to survive from glucose.

CARBOHYDRATES, ATP, AND MUSCLE CONTRACTION

What we've established thus far is the fact that the first ten seconds of Static Contraction exercise require "zero" in the way of food sources, the reason being the presence of ATP stores in the body and the ability of CP stores to create more ATP. After this ten-second point, however, the anaerobic system kicks in with carbohydrates as the primary source of fuel and manufactures its own ATP for at least the next ten seconds (in fact, it remains in this mode up until about 50 seconds into the set, at which point the aerobic system begins to kick in).

What we intend to do with the Golfer's Two-Minute Workout is to engage in a purely anaerobic activity—at the highest possible level of intensity—in order to make maximum gains in strength.

Now, all of this is well and good, but what happens when the intensity of an exercise is at (or even near) maximal levels during the 10–20 second anaerobic timeframe is that the anaerobic system—in an effort to meet the increased demand for ATP—is suddenly forced to break down large amounts of glucose (from any form of carbohydrate) to form large quantities of pyruvic acid, which can only be blown off by engaging the aerobic system (which converts the pyruvic acid into a compound called acetyl co-A, which is then readily dispersed by the system). And since the Golfer's Two-Minute Workout attempts to prevent the aerobic system from becoming a factor in the equation, the bulk of the pyruvic acid is chemically transformed into another chemical called lactic acid or lactate.

What happens when lactic acid forms is, essentially, the "beginning of the end"—at least in terms of the ability of your muscles to continue contracting. Your muscles and the enzymes that comprise and surround them can only withstand a small amount of lactate before the acid starts to shut down the contraction process. When you train a very high level of intensity within the anaerobic pathways, your muscles will begin to burn and eventually your contraction will cease. To review: ATP is created through anaerobic (and also the aerobic) systems and is required to allow the actin and myosin proteins to fulfill their contractile/relaxation functions. If you exceed your ATP production capacity, the set is over.

FIBER TYPES

Not to complicate matters, but you ought to know that there exist several different types of actin and myosin filaments. In fact, the speed with which a muscle can contract is ultimately dependent upon the type of myosin contained within the muscle. Heavy meromyosin (HMM) is recruited for rapid ATP breakdown and is found in powerful, fast muscles. Conversely, light meromyosin (LMM) is a requisite of slower, more endurance-related muscles.

Human anatomy and physiology studies have revealed that there exist four distinct fiber types in our species. Talk to most would-be experts or personal trainers and you'll hear a very simplified (and scientifically incorrect) synopsis that there exist only fast-twitch and slow-twitch muscles. Fast muscle fibers differ from their slower cousins in many ways, endurance-capacity being one of them. In fact, it's in the endurance area rather than in the velocity or speed department that their differences become most apparent. The fast-oxidative (FO) fibers have relatively good endurance (the term "oxidative" refers solely to the aerobic machinery within the fast-oxidative fiber itself). Another fast-twitch fiber is the fast-glycolytic (FG), which is very fast in contracting, and very powerful but has nothing to offer in the way of endurance (the term "glycolytic" refers to the anaerobic machinery within the fast-glycolytic fiber itself). As an example, the huge deltoids and massive triceps and biceps of bodybuilders are comprised almost entirely of FG fibers.

Intermediate in speed, endurance, and power are the fast-oxidative-glycolytic (FOG) fibers, which contain both the anaerobic and aerobic machinery within their cellular makeup. On the other side of the coin, slow muscle (type-S), so called because in comparison with, say, FG fibers, type-S fibers seem slow, is an endurance fiber used primarily by those who engage in distance activities. It's very powerful aerobically, with lots of aerobic enzymes, blood vessels, and myoglobin (an oxygen-storing endurance compound). On the down side, however, these types of fibers aren't capable of creating much force and, consequently, don't possess the inherent mass potential of their quicker cousins.

THE GENETIC FACTOR

All right, so what does all of this mean? Well, for those of us with an athletic bent, our fiber type percentages and distribution appear to be genetically predetermined—a product of breeding as opposed to environmental influences, if you will. Still, most of us are brought into the world with a more or less even distribution of all types of fibers—both fast and slow twitch. This is not good if you want to be a powerlifter, as obviously a higher complement of FG fibers would be of greater benefit here—but then, fortunately, most of us were born to be golfers, not weightlifters. As a result, premier powerlifters have a high FG fiber percentage, while the average man usually has a greater complement of type-S fibers.

The Golfer's Two-Minute Workout and Muscle-Fiber Recruitment

Now that we understand how muscles contract, we need to understand the role of muscle-fiber recruitment as it pertains to training with the Golfer's Two-Minute Workout. The brain tends to recruit more fibers as it perceives the need for them. This is accomplished via the brain's motor nerves, which, in keeping with the dictates of the brain, follow a relatively fixed order in their recruitment process. The process involves only the precise amount of electrical current necessary to turn on the selected muscle fibers.

Of the four fiber types, the type-S, or slow fibers, are the easiest to engage, as they don't require a lot of current. Slightly more juice is required to engage the FO fibers and more still for the FOGs. The ones that require the highest electrical output to engage are the FGs. It's important to remember this fact while you are experiencing the lactic acid slowly building up in the muscle you're training—it may help you to stick it out for the full 10 to 20 seconds. The reason for this is that the brain is in no hurry to hit the switch for those FG fibers—the ones you want to stimulate for strength increases that will parlay into a longer drive on the fairway. The brain would rather engage the least amount necessary to accomplish a given task. After all, the brain is an organ of survival, and conserving energy was (particularly in the early days of our species' existence), and still is, essential for the long-term survival of our species.

Anyway, the brain will first attempt to accomplish the sustained contraction of a given muscle with only the type-S fibers. When these soon become inadequate to sustain the contraction, the brain will recruit the FOs and shortly thereafter the FOG fibers to assist with the task. If these fail, and they will, the brain will have realized that it needs far and away more firepower than it's been providing, and only then will it send out the signal to engage the elusive FG fibers. This process is known in physiology circles as "Orderly Recruitment," for the brain does not engage in the firing up of random fibers.

Now it should become clear from the aforementioned that the brain, when recruiting muscle fibers, doesn't concern itself with issues of velocity—only force requirements. It has no concern with how fast you want to lift a weight or how quick you wish to run—remember, it cannot randomly recruit muscle fibers. Instead, the brain ascertains the precise force required to accomplish the task at hand and recruits only the precise amount of muscle fibers accordingly. An interesting aspect of this phenomenon is that when the brain sends sufficient current to activate the FG fibers in a Static Contraction set, we automatically know that the type-S, FOs, and FOG fibers—that is, *all* available muscle fibers—have been activated and engaged, thereby ensuring maximum muscle fiber stimulation.

THE CONQUEST OF IGNORANCE

The facts of the matter regarding muscle fiber recruitment by the brain obviously fly in the face of what some of the personal trainers and strength coaches have been preaching regarding plyometrics and other such "explosive" movements for developing quicker follow-through on your drive, or even for increasing your strength.

Their theories, that the "fast-twitch" muscle fibers can only be activated by performing various exercises as fast as you possibly can, completely disregard the principles of motor control and muscle fiber recruitment. First off, if you try to train by utilizing a very high rate of speed and ballistic movements, you'll be forced to use light weights, since the heavier the resistance, the slower one can move it. If you use a light weight, the brain immediately picks up on the *force* required to move that weight and, obviously, with a light weight the current required to generate enough *force* to move the resistance at a high speed would be only sufficient to engage the type-S and maybe the FO fibers. The FG fibers—the ones most important to high-speed movement and the ones most responsible for increases in size and strength—are never activated in such a system because the resistance you're required to lift, and the force you're required to generate to do so, isn't sufficient to warrant the brain sending the signal to recruit the FGs and thereby engage the full complement of muscle fibers.

Not only does ballistic or plyometric training not stimulate the muscle fibers the way its theory suggests, but it only involves half of the muscle fibers available to be stimulated in any given set. Obviously, if you're only stimulating half the fibers you could be, your training system is only half as efficient as it could be, and certainly only half as efficient as one that engages all of the available fibers.

Furthermore, when are the majority of muscle fibers involved in any given movement? Answer: when the target muscle group is in a position of full contraction. The longer the muscle is maximally contracted, the more muscle fibers are recruited (right down to the FG fibers). Any training system that is predicated on heaving weights up and down ballistically doesn't even come close to bringing the target muscle group into a position of full muscular contraction for any meaningful length of time and certainly will not engage anywhere near the full complement of available muscle fibers.

As if that wasn't enough, such training is highly traumatic to your joints and connective tissues. A barbell weighing 100 pounds, for example, if curled slowly in the conventional fashion will provide 100 pounds of resistance both concentrically and eccentrically (up and down). Holding 100 pounds statically in a position of full muscular contraction will do likewise. However, jerking and heaving that same 100 pound barbell up and down will magnify the trauma force on the joints to well over 1,000 pounds—and the impact to the joints, which must suddenly stretch and then ballistically extend muscles, tendons, ligaments, and muscle fascia, can quickly add up to injury. High-speed training is dangerous and far less productive than the Golfer's Two-Minute Workout, featuring Static Contraction training.

Chapter 9

NUTRITION FOR OPTIMUM PERFORMANCE

The Golfer's Two-Minute Workout places unusual stress on the body's various biochemical reserves. These reserves include the amino acid pool (which is of vital significance since amino acids are the very stuff of life—and of stronger muscles); the elements sodium and potassium, electrolytes needed for high-intensity muscle contraction; those important minerals calcium and magnesium, which help maintain a steady-state nervous system; not to mention vitamins, which transform our food into the enzymes responsible for energy metabolism.

The nutrients mentioned above are but a few that go into making up a well-balanced diet. Without an ample supply each day of protein, vitamins, minerals, fats, carbohydrates, and water, your workouts will inevitably degenerate into pointless affairs, full of sound and fury perhaps, but ultimately signifying nothing.

THE VARIOUS NUTRIENTS

The first consideration in fueling your golfing machine is health. Along with adequate rest, maintaining a well-balanced diet is absolutely essential in becoming a better golfer. Balancing your diet for health maintenance and for muscle gains requires over 40 different nutrients. These various nutrients can be obtained from generous daily portions of the four basic food groups, or what is now referred to as the food pyramid:

1. CEREALS AND GRAINS

2. FRUITS AND VEGETABLES

3. MILK AND DAIRY PRODUCTS

4. MEAT, FISH, AND POULTRY

The various nutrients are classified within the six major categories already mentioned: protein, vitamins, minerals, fats, carbohydrates, and water. The following analysis will help you understand the role of each in your golfer's diet:

Protein: The word protein is from the Greek, meaning prime or chief. After water (the primary constituent of muscle tissue), protein makes up the bulk of the contractile element within muscle tissue.

Carbohydrates: The primary fuel source of our muscles comes from carbohydrates, in the simple form known as glucose. When we don't take in enough sugar through our diets to fuel muscular contractions, our bodies transform the amino acid alanine, derived from ingested protein of our own muscle tissue, into glucose. So carbohydrates have a protein-sparing effect. In addition to supplying energy, carbohydrates supply important building blocks of life as well. Deribose, found in RNA and DNA (two essential components of all living matter), is a form of sugar and is derived from the carbohydrates we eat. Carbohydrates stored within our muscles in the form of glycogen are largely responsible for keeping water inside their cells.

Fats: Fats are an important source of fuel and provide energy in low-intensity endurance activities when the more limited glycogen reserves have been depleted. Since certain vitamins are soluble only in fat, it is obvious that fats figure crucially in a well-balanced diet.

Vitamins and Minerals: All the various vitamins and minerals are referred to as micronutrients, as they are required in such small quantities each day. Recommended daily allowances of the micronutrients are measured in milligrams, as opposed to the grams of the macronutrients. Vitamins and minerals are combined in the body to form the enzymes that serve as catalysts in innumerable physiological processes. If you are consuming a well-balanced diet, you could be getting all the vitamins and minerals you need. If, however, there is any doubt as to whether your diet is balanced, by all means take a general vitamin-mineral supplement.

Water: All of life's complex chemical processes take place in a fluid medium provided by water. The fluidity of our blood and lymph is water; water is the waste remover through urine and excrement; it keeps our joints lubricated and helps maintain a constant body temperature; and, not of least importance to the golfer, water is the primary constituent of muscle tissue. Viewed thusly, water could rightly be said to be the most important nutrient for survival as well as for growth. Drinking more water and fluids than thirst dictates is not going to hasten the muscle strengthening process, however. The body will absorb only what it needs for maintenance and that little bit of growth you might be stimulating on a daily basis—and will excrete the rest.

EATING MORE ISN'T THE ANSWER

While it is important for the aspiring golfer to take in appropriate amounts of the nutrients listed above, eating more food than you need will not cause your muscles to become stronger at a faster rate. Most of us make the mistake of believing that muscle is made up of protein, and that you have to eat lots of it to build stronger muscles. However, as indicated above, it just so happens that muscle comprises 70% water, 22% protein, and 6 to 8% lipids and inorganic materials. From this we can readily discern that the primary constituent of muscle is not protein—as the advertisements that sell protein would have you believe—but water. However, this does not mean that we hasten the strength development process by drinking inordinate amounts of water every day. For reasons that we've already touched upon above, your body eliminates excess water through urination. You don't have the same impunity with protein, however, because protein contains calories and when you eat more calories than you need to maintain your existing condition, the excess (apart from that which can be excreted) is stored as fat. It is interesting to note that protein can make you just as fat as carbohydrates or fat do because protein contains calories, and it is the excess calories—no matter what their source—that makes your fat.

THE IDEAL DIET FOR GOLFERS

Let's assume that you're going to be able to apply the principles espoused in this book successfully enough to stimulate ten pounds of lean tissue and lose ten pounds of body fat over the coming year. Obviously such an exchange would not register on a body-weight scale, but you would notice a huge difference in both your appearance and in your performance on the links. And while nutrition must factor into creating those ten additional pounds, the question becomes, to what extent? In other words, just how much food will you have to eat in order to gain those ten pounds of pure muscle without adding any body fat?

Well, first of all, you've got to recognize that one pound of muscle tissue contains 600 calories. This is true in all human beings, whether it be yourself or the current Master's champion. If you were to surgically excise a pound of muscle tissue and place it in a device known as a calorimeter, it would give off 600 calories of heat. Now, if you were to gain ten pounds of muscle mass over the course of one year, you would have to consume 10 × 600 calories or 6,000 a year over and above your maintenance need of calories (that is, the amount of calories consumed on a daily basis that are required to simply maintain your current body weight). You read that correctly; that's 6,000 extra calories a year—not 6,000 extra calories a day, a week, or a month—but 6,000 extra calories a year! And eating that amount within a day, a week, or a month will do nothing at all to hasten the muscle growth process. Again, your body has specific nutritional requirements and any amount above these requirements is passed off or stored as fat.

Still, the tendency for most golfers is to think of their nutritional needs in terms of days. And if we do the math on this, we find that the daily total of extra nutrition required to grow those extra ten pounds of muscle comes out to approximately 16 extra calories (i.e., 6,000 calories divided by 365 days) over and above your daily maintenance need of calories.

It should be pointed out that the actual process of eating contributes nothing to the growth process. The primary requisite for muscle growth is stimulation, which is done with your Static Contraction training in the gym. Once this has occurred, nutrition becomes a secondary requisite in that you must provide adequate nutrition to maintain your existing physical mass, and then you've got to provide those extra 16 calories or so to allow for that tiny bit of extra muscle growth that might be taking place on a daily basis—and we want to emphasize "might be taking place."

The fact is that most golfers—regardless of their training preference—already eat more than they need to gain an additional ten pounds of muscle over the course of a year. If you're not gaining strength presently and you're eating sufficiently, then the reason you're not growing is that you're not training with sufficient intensity to stimulate an adaptive muscular response. So, the formula again is: Stimulate growth through your high-intensity training and then eat enough to maintain your existing physical mass—your "maintenance need of calories"—and then, to assist in the growth of those additional ten pounds, you've got to tack on an additional 16 calories a day to your maintenance need of calories.

DETERMINING YOUR MAINTENANCE NEED OF CALORIES

Some of you reading this book may be asking yourself, "What is a maintenance need of calories, and how do I determine it?" Well, your maintenance need of calories is simply that: the amount of calories required to maintain you at your present body weight. The method required to ascertain this is very simple.

Every day for five days write down every single thing you eat—from the cream you put in your coffee to the ketchup you put on your french fries—and then, after each day is over, sit down with a calorie counting book and calculate your total number of calories for that day. Follow this procedure for five days and then, at the end of the five days, total up your five daily caloric totals and divide that number by five. Voila! You've just computed your maintenance need of calories. Here's a hypothetical example of how this might break down:

MONDAY: YOU CONSUME A TOTAL OF 2,500 CALORIES.

TUESDAY: YOU CONSUME A TOTAL OF 2,700 CALORIES.

WEDNESDAY: IT'S THE MIDDLE OF THE WEEK—A BAD WEEK, LET US SUPPOSE—AND YOUR HANDICAP JUST WENT INTO THE TRIPLE DIGITS. YOU GET ANGRY AND FRUSTRATED AND PIG OUT AND CONSUME 4,500 CALORIES.

THURSDAY: YOU'RE NOW FEELING GUILTY FOR YOUR DIETARY ABERRATION THE DAY BEFORE AND, TO ATONE FOR YOUR MISDEED, YOU ONLY HAVE 1,500 CALORIES.

FRIDAY: THINGS ARE BACK TO NORMAL IN YOUR LIFE—NOW YOUR ONLY HANDICAP IS YOUR PERSONALITY—SO YOUR DAILY INTAKE IS 2,500 CALORIES.

Now take these five totals and add them up, which, in this instance, comes out to 13,700 calories total for the five days. Now divide this number by five (the number of days) and your resulting daily average is 2,740 calories per day. This is your maintenance need of calories, assuming of course that you neither gained nor lost weight during the time you recorded these figures.

This simple method of computing your maintenance need of calories takes into account such diverse and highly individual factors as your basal metabolic rate (BMR) and your voluntary physical activity output. It doesn't even matter how unique or fast your individual metabolism is—it's all taken into account with this formula.

Once your maintenance need of calories has been determined by this method, it becomes a relatively simple procedure to add 16 extra calories a day to your daily average in order to provide that extra nutrition necessary to assist in the growth process particular to those extra ten pounds of pure muscle. With our above hypothetical example, this would mean that the daily average caloric intake would be increased from 2,740 to 2,756 per day. And those extra 16 calories can be obtained by simply taking two bites out of an apple!

All this simply underscores the fact that force-feeding yourself hundreds or even thousands of extra calories per day is not going to hasten the strength building process at all. In fact, the only thing that force-feeding will succeed in hastening is an increase in the size of your waistline. The most important requisite in building stronger muscles to help you on the golf course is simply stimulating a strength increase through your efforts in the gym. Then, stay out of the gym and eat a well-balanced diet.

Chapter 10

OTHER TRAINING
CONSIDERATIONS
FOR GOLFERS

The data that we presented in this study reveals some startling implications. For one thing, it would appear that a lot less training is required for golfers to improve their game than even most "experts" would have believed previously.

According to the data, a proper training methodology, such as the Golfer's Two-Minute Workout, featuring maximal static contractions of 10 to 20 seconds each, is all that is necessary to stimulate maximum strength gains for the purpose of improving your golf game and stimulating an increase in strength and power.

This data fits perfectly into the 10- to 60-second anaerobic pathway necessary for optimum increases in strength to occur. And, assuming two separate workouts of six exercises each (for a total of 12 exercises to cover all of the body's major muscle groups) and assuming only a ten-second hold, it makes for a total workout time for each workout of one minute—maximum! Or, on the other hand, if you decide to go for broke, and make use of the full measure of anaerobic energy available, your workout could last a mere two minutes!

Also revealed by the data presented is that muscular tension is the sole factor responsible for stimulating strength increases and muscle growth. That's correct; it isn't repetitions, it isn't long workouts, and it isn't training your muscle from a host of different angles—it's tension. And the Golfer's Two-Minute Workout, as we've explained it, creates the highest possible level of tension, and hence strength stimulation, within a given muscle. It has to. After all, your muscles are being trained solely in the fully contracted position, that one position in a muscle's potential range of motion where all of its fibers are activated maximally, thereby creating the greatest contractile force or muscle tension.

THE THREE PHASES OF MUSCLE-GROWTH STIMULATION

One of the most important facets of strength training is the fact that it is "tri-phasic" in nature. In order for your muscles to become stronger, you must do the following:

- **STIMULATE AN ADAPTIVE STRENGTHENING RESPONSE WITHIN THE MUSCLE AT A CELLULAR LEVEL.**

- **ALLOW TIME TO PASS IN ORDER FOR YOUR MUSCLES TO RECOVER FROM THE WORKOUT.**

- **ALLOW STILL MORE TIME TO PASS IN ORDER FOR YOUR CENTRAL NERVOUS SYSTEM TO RECOVER AND FOR YOUR MUSCULAR RESERVES TO OVERCOMPENSATE OR GROW STRONGER.**

If this sounds rather simple, it's only because it is. And yet this is one of the most frequently misunderstood and neglected facets of strength training as practiced by golfers. The process whereby you increase your strength is tri-phasic, and, even if you neglect only one of these three phases, you will never realize any progress, despite your greatest efforts in the gym.

Allow us to elaborate: In order for an increase in your strength to occur, it must first be stimulated at the cellular level. This can only be done by imposing a stress or demand of the highest physiological order. Mild effort won't cut it. It is through high-tensile muscular contraction that the intensity or stress upon a muscle can be increased to the point where it is perceived by the central nervous system as a call to arms to defend the body's limited supply of muscular energy reserves. And the only way the body can accomplish this is by enlarging upon its existing muscle mass stores. The higher the intensity, the greater the growth stimulation, pure and simple. For example, walking will stimulate more strength increases in the body than will sitting, simply because the intensity of walking is greater than the intensity of sitting. Jogging, on the other hand, will stimulate more strength gains than walking, again, because the intensity of jogging is greater than that of walking (note also that you can spend much more time walking, due to its low-intensity nature, than you can jogging). Sprinting will stimulate far and away more strength gains than jogging because of its ultrahigh-intensity nature; consequently, the time spent engaged in an all-out sprint will, again, because of its higher level of intensity, be extremely brief. Whereas you can walk for days and jog for hours, you can only engage in an all-out sprint for a matter of seconds, and yet those mere seconds will have stimulated more of an adaptive response, in terms of increased strength in your legs, than all the hours of walking and jogging combined.

And so it is with the Golfer's Two-Minute Workout. In fact, the intensity level of the Golfer's Two-Minute Workout far exceeds that of sprinting in terms of muscle fiber stimulation. After all, when you've finished an all-out sprint, you are still capable of jogging at an easy pace for miles, if need be. Whereas after one

all-out set of Static Contraction leg extensions, your thigh muscles will have been taken to the point where they can no longer sustain a full contraction and their fibers can no longer function. As a result, some time is required to pass before you can even stand, let alone walk! Such a phenomenon is an obvious indicator that a far greater degree of muscle fiber recruitment, involvement, and stimulation has taken place. More so, in fact, than can be found in any other form of conventional exercise.

Again, if you attempt to train before you have fully recovered and overcompensated from your previous workout, all you will succeed in doing is prolong the recovery process, as you would then have to recover from your present training session in addition to the antecedent one. And, if you allow enough time for recovery to take place but not enough time for growth to occur, you still won't grow! Why? Because it takes time for the growth process to be switched on. No one is exempt from this basic law of biology—not you, me, or Greg Norman.

It's not unlike the process of hair growth; that is, it is a biological process that cannot be rushed. You could go into a hair salon every day and have your hair "professionally" washed, styled, blow-dried, or cut—but that won't hasten the hair growth process, which, being biological in nature, cannot be affected by anything other than your DNA. When I refer to this process, I am of course referring to the recovery of the physical system as a whole. Localized muscle recovery, as touched upon earlier, can take place quite rapidly in certain individuals, but that still doesn't alter the fact that complete systemic recovery always precedes the final growth process. This last block of time is the most important requisite in the overcompensation or "muscle growth" process, apart from the initial strength stimulation itself. Of course, if you train with low intensity, you might well be able to recover sufficiently to train again the next day, but your progress in terms of strength gains will be minimal. And your objective as a golfer should never be to see how much exercise you can tolerate, but rather to see just how little exercise is required to stimulate maximum increases in muscle size and strength, which is solely a product of training intensity.

With this in mind then, the most effective training routine would be one that is obviously of the highest possible intensity for maximum growth stimulation and of comparatively brief duration. For example, let us assume that you have trained with sufficient intensity to stimulate the cellular call to arms for additional strength increases. We'll call this Phase One. At this point, you must forget about training entirely so that you can enter Phase Two, the stage of recovery. An individual muscle may, in some cases, recover fully within 24 hours and, in some extremely rare individuals, within even one hour. However, the recuperative subsystems that feed the body and serve to mediate the recovery and growth processes require far more time to recover from the exhaustive and depleting effects of a growth-stimulating training session, and this amount will vary —in some cases quite widely—among golfers.

After identical workouts, for example, one golfer may be able to return to the gym in 48 hours and note a strength improvement, while another golfer may need as many as eight weeks to go by in order to simply recover from his previous workout, and then another block of time on top of that to allow for the growth he stimulated in that one workout eight weeks previously to manifest. Hard to believe, you say? Consider the following: The May 1993 issue of the *Journal of Physiology* reported that a group of men and women aged 22 to 32 took part in an exercise experiment in which they trained their forearms in a negative-only fashion to a point of muscular failure. (Negative-only training means that instead of simply raising and lowering the weight, which is called "positive" and "negative" movement respectively, the trainee has someone else lift the weight for him and then concentrates solely on the lowering, or "negative," aspect of the repetition.) Negatives are considered by some exercise physiologists to be more important than positive or concentric contractions, owing to the fact that more weight is able to be employed. In any event, all of the subjects agreed that they were most sore two days after exercising, and that the soreness was gone by the ninth day. But it took most of the people nearly six weeks to regain just half of the strength they had before the workout!

The study concluded that muscles are drained far more severely by intense exercise than was previously thought. According to this research, it can literally take months for the muscles of some individuals to heal and adapt after an intensive workout. Regardless of what your personal range of recovery happens to be, one thing is certain: Everyone's personal recovery ability takes much longer to complete itself than was initially thought, and training more than two days a week—and maybe even more than once a week—is going to be a mistake for most golfers who are looking to increase the strength of their muscles.

Should you opt to train again—even though your muscles "feel fine"—within the 72-hour time frame, then the only thing you will have accomplished will be diminished results. Recovery always precedes growth in terms of strength, and it will not take place unless your muscles and the subsystems that feed them have completely recovered. It is crucial to never let your enthusiasm work against your objectives.

Phase Three, the actual phase in which the increase in strength manifests, will take place, so science tells us, within a 10- to 15-minute time period after complete systemic recovery has taken

place. It must be stressed that intense muscular contraction—
the only kind of training stimulus that results in immediate
muscular adaptation—is a form of stress to the muscles and the
overall physical system. When performed properly, such
training will stimulate a compensatory buildup in the form of
additional muscle strength, which aids the body in coping
more successfully with a stressor of like severity in the future.

We can conclude from the above data that a golfer's ideal
routine would be one of the highest possible contractile intensity (and because of this fact, of the briefest possible duration)
to stimulate muscular growth and would occur infrequently
enough to allow for recovery and growth to take place once
stimulated.

If, like some golfers, you adopt a more conventional strength
training program, wherein you end up training a different body
part each day, the muscles you've trained may well have recovered by the time of your next workout. But if you do then train
again, you'll only be making daily inroads into your systemic
recovery, which, ultimately, feeds and dictates your future
levels of muscular strength. This physiological fact reveals to us
that daily training for the purpose of increasing the strength of
our muscles is a mistake because it doesn't allow for recovery—
let alone growth—to take place.

The golfers (and there are a few of them) who insist on training
six to seven days a week (whether on a three days on/one day
off or four days on/one day off system) will all witness a
decompensatory effect, as the resulting drain on the regulatory
subsystems of the body will actually prevent the buildup of
muscle strength. In fact, all the energy reserves will have to be
called upon simply to attempt to overcome the energy debt
caused by such overtraining.

Chapter 11

QUESTIONS AND ANSWERS

DO I NEED A PARTNER
TO PERFORM THIS WORKOUT?

The relevant issue here is having a way to hold weights in
your strongest range and not to let them descend into your
weak range, which could cause an injury. A partner is a great
help in this regard, as he can assist you with lifting the
weights in and out of your weak range. The other proven

benefit of having a partner is the psychological boost of
having someone cheer you on to greater performance. For
some people, the value of that cannot be understated.

It is also possible to train without a partner by using a power
rack, Smith machine, or other device that limits the position of
the weight being used. These units physically prevent a weight
from moving into your weak range. Probably the best-case

**THIS SMITH MACHINE PERFORMS THE SAME FUNCTION
AS A POWER RACK IN LIMITING THE RANGE OF MOTION
OF MANY EXERCISES.**

scenario is to use the above equipment and to have an encouraging training partner—that's the best of both worlds.

● ▬▬ ▬▬ ▬▬ ▬▬ ▬▬ ●

I DON'T HAVE ALL THE EQUIPMENT I NEED. CAN I SUBSTITUTE EXERCISES?

If you don't train in a commercial gym, it will be a rare case to have all of the equipment used for these exercises in your home. Frankly, you will probably still do about as well as the subjects

THERE IS NOTHING TO PREVENT YOU FROM SUBSTITUTING A FAVORITE EXERCISE, LIKE THIS SEATED PRESS, AND ADAPTING IT TO A STRONG-RANGE STATIC HOLD TECHNIQUE.

in our study if you substitute some exercises or even if you drop one or two of them altogether.

We have suggested some alternate exercises, and there is nothing preventing you from taking a favorite exercise and adapting it to a strong-range static-hold technique. Choose exercises that provide maximum overload to the muscle being targeted and keep increasing the intensity. There is research to show that exercising one muscle group can increase strength in seemingly unrelated muscles because muscle growth is controlled by the entire central nervous system. Therefore it may be possible to design a workout with fewer exercises that still delivers functional strength throughout the body. So if you are going to drop some exercises and substitute others, try to use exercises that involve as many muscles as possible in a single exercise rather than the conventional method of multiple "isolation" exercises for individual muscles.

CAN I AUGMENT THE GOLFER'S TWO-MINUTE WORKOUT WITH CONVENTIONAL STRENGTH TRAINING?

Not really. The Golfer's Two-Minute Workout was designed to be as efficient as possible. It uses maximum intensity and minimum duration. Adding extra exercises, especially if they are performed in a conventional reps and sets manner, greatly increases the duration at the expense of intensity. Furthermore, there is only so much growth or improvement that can be stimulated on any given day, and there is ample reason to believe that the Golfer's Two-Minute Workout will be stimulating about all it can in just one or two minutes. To use our haircut analogy yet again, performing the Golfer's Two-Minute Workout followed by a conventional workout would be a bit like getting your hair cut at one salon, then walking to another salon to get it cut again—just to make sure you get the benefit of two good stylists.

I'VE BEEN TRAINING FOR A FEW WEEKS AND I'M FINDING THAT MY STRENGTH EXCEEDS THE CAPACITY OF THE EQUIPMENT I'M USING. WHAT SHOULD I DO?

Believe it or not, this is a very common problem for people who train with strong-range exercises. As a rule, pulling

PULLING MOVEMENTS CAN OFTEN BE DONE UNILATERALLY, OR ONE ARM OR LEG AT A TIME, WHICH EFFECTIVELY DOUBLES THE WEIGHT OF THE EQUIPMENT.

movements can often be done unilaterally, or one arm or leg at a time, which effectively doubles the weight of the equipment. Although the manufacturers would never approve, it is also sometimes possible to add weight in the form of plates or dumbbells to certain pieces of equipment in order to increase the weight stack. We had to resort to this during this study. (Which is why, if you have a really keen eye, you may have noticed that some workouts in the study were over two minutes. It takes extra seconds to perform the same exercise one arm or leg at a time.)

Free weights are probably the best solution to this problem, as they allow the addition of weight up to levels that most people will never achieve and that golfers probably don't need anyway.

WILL AN INCREASE IN STRENGTH AND/OR MUSCLE MASS INTERFERE WITH THE GEOMETRY OF MY GOLF SWING?

This seems to be a common belief that permeates many sports. Swimmers, boxers, and martial artists, to name only a few, often worry about becoming "muscle-bound" and unable to move with freedom or fluidity. This belief is (as lawyers say) groundless and without merit. All the movement in your body, from a powerful drive to the wink of an eye, is done by muscles. Increased muscle tone, power, and even size only serve you better in all these movements. It is a rare golfer, indeed, who has the musculature of a gymnast or a ballet dancer, and yet these athletes are the models of grace and fluidity of movement. How ironic it is that people have come to view five pounds of extra muscle as a liability yet never ask how five pounds of extra fat will limit their movement— which it will. Gain muscle mass and strength and the geometry of your swing will improve, not decline.

WOULD I GET MORE BENEFIT FROM PERFORMING TWO OR THREE "SETS" OF 10- TO 20-SECOND STATIC HOLDS?

We did a study of strong-range Static Contraction training with a large group of bodybuilders and found that a second "set" of static holds added about 10% to their strength gains. Performing a third set yielded results slightly worse than one or two sets. Performing the second set represents 100% more work for 10% more benefit, which offends our sense of efficiency. Also, we suspect that over the course of several months to a year this narrow improvement would diminish. Since our interest lies in the scientific discipline of efficiency, our work in the future is more likely to focus on how to create not a four-minute workout but a one-minute workout.

I AM A TOTAL BEGINNER AT STRENGTH TRAINING AND WEIGHT LIFTING. WILL THE GOLFER'S TWO-MINUTE WORKOUT BE TOO INTENSE FOR ME TO START WITH?

No. The physiological principles that govern strength increases are the same for everyone. If you read the comments of test subject Laura G., you saw that she was a newcomer to weight training at the beginning of this study. Yet she improved her overall strength by 107% over six workouts that were identical to everyone else's on the study. Although a beginner uses lighter weights, he or she is still straining maximally to hold those weights for 10 to 20 seconds. A newcomer straining to hold 20 pounds gets the same muscle-stimulating benefit as a bodybuilder straining to hold 300 pounds—as long as they are both operating a maximal exertion.

IF THE GOLFER'S TWO-MINUTE WORKOUT IS SO EFFECTIVE AT INCREASING STRENGTH, WILL IT CREATE LARGE, BULGING MUSCLES THAT I DO NOT WISH TO HAVE?

The truth is that large, bulging muscles not only take a long time to create, but they also will not sneak up on you unexpectedly. The Golfer's Two-Minute Workout has the capability to take you to the limits of your genetic potential, so if you want large, bulging muscles, it can deliver them—eventually. Most golfers, however, will increase their strength and muscle tone to a point that they are satisfied with, then switch to a maintenance mode. A maintenance mode is simply achieved by performing workouts that are *not* progressive on a regular schedule. You simply go to the gym every two, four, or six weeks and perform the same workout as you did the last time. This will keep you at your present levels of strength, and you need not fear becoming more muscular than you desire.

HOW LONG CAN I EXPECT TO SEE STEADY INCREASES IN MY STRENGTH?

It depends on your definition of "steady." The fastest *rate* of improvement will be seen in the first two to four months of your training. After that the rate of improvement might slow down, but it will still be steady in that you will not hit plateaus or begin to lose strength—unless you overtrain. The absolute key to *steady* progress is to adjust your frequency of training. If your workouts are far enough apart you will be fully recovered when you return to the gym, and you will make a little more progress. The rate will not stay fixed, but progress can be steady for years.

HOW LONG SHOULD I REST BETWEEN EXERCISES?

This is a question that comes up very frequently. As usual we do not offer a cookie-cutter answer. It would be easy to say, "Rest 40 seconds between each exercise for best results." But the truth is that the amount of rest a person requires is dependent on many factors, such as age, gender, level of conditioning, and more. A twenty-year-old who has been training for two years will probably require less rest between sets than a fifty-year-old who is training for the first time. (See how irresponsible the "cookie-cutter" answer guys are?) The principle that must always be kept in mind is forcing your muscles to perform the highest amount of work per unit of time. In short, the rest between exercises should be as brief as possible but as long as necessary. That might be 15 seconds or 3 minutes.

WHEN IS A STATIC REP FINISHED?

The objective of statically holding a weight is to hold the weight motionless in space. Once the weight begins to descend, the rep is over. This is an important distinction to make because when a weight is descending all we know for certain is that you are pushing with insufficient force to hold the weight stationary. But we do not know exactly how insufficient. One pound? Ten pounds? Leaving the clock running during this period of unknown measurement would greatly sacrifice precision. The clock stops when the weight starts to drop.

I WAS PERFORMING THE GOLFER'S TWO-MINUTE WORKOUT IN MY LOCAL GYM AND A PERSONAL TRAINER TOLD ME THAT THE "LAW OF SPECIFICITY OF TRAINING" SAYS THAT STATIC CONTRACTION EXERCISE CANNOT YIELD INCREASES IN MY FULL-RANGE STRENGTH. DON'T I NEED FULL-RANGE STRENGTH FOR GOLFING?

This is a very common belief that many people feel is supported by a valid theory. The Specific Adaptation to Imposed Demands

(SAID) principle of physiology is valid and well established. Briefly, this principle states that the body will adapt itself in a manner that is appropriate to the demands or stress that are placed upon it. It should be noted, however, that this law states that there will be a specificity of adaptation but *not* an *exclusivity* of adaptation. If the body responded with an exclusive adaptation to imposed demands (EAID?), then a person who lifted weights through a full range of motion for many years would have no static strength whatsoever because he had never imposed a static demand on his muscles. The converse would also be true; a person who trained for many years with only static contractions and was very muscular would be incapable of moving the lightest weight through any range of motion. It is obvious that the body does not operate this way. While there is conclusive evidence of a specificity of adaptation, it is by no means an exclusivity.

Corroboration of this can be seen in our own study with bodybuilders, who, on average, had a 51.3% increase in static strength over a ten-week period but "only" a 27.6% and 34.3% increase, respectively, in their full-range dynamic strength of one-rep and ten-rep maximums. So the imposed demand of static contractions provided an increase in strength that was more specific to static strength than to dynamic strength but still greatly improved their dynamic strength. Yes, golfers need full-range strength, and the Golfer's Two-Minute Workout delivers it.

HAS THERE EVER BEEN A STUDY PROVING THAT A FULL RANGE OF MOTION IS NECESSARY IN ORDER TO STIMULATE MUSCLE GROWTH?

No. And there never will be.

It may seem as though I am recklessly predicting the outcome of future scientific experiments by saying that there never will be a study that proves a full range of motion is necessary to stimulate muscle growth. In fact, however, I am correct with the highest order of certainty. First of all, our own experience with static contractions revealed that exercising with zero range of motion would stimulate substantial new muscle growth and strength increases. You cannot have one valid study that says a zero range will stimulate muscle growth and a second valid study that says only a 100% range of motion will stimulate growth. Second, outside of the gym, virtually none of the six billion people on the planet use a full range of motion when going about their daily activities, and yet these people are all able to increase their muscle mass. For example, climbing stairs will increase the strength in your legs, even though a six-inch step is nowhere near a full range of leg motion. It is perfectly rational to conclude that there never will be a study that will prove a full range of motion is an indispensable requirement for muscle growth, just as there will never be a study proving that eating kiwi is an indispensable requirement for muscle growth.

I WANT TO GAIN STRENGTH AND LOSE FAT. CAN I MIX CARDIO WORKOUTS WITH STRENGTH WORKOUTS AND NOT OVERTRAIN?

This is another of the most common questions that we receive. The lack of good information on this subject still continues to amaze me. Aerobic training to lose fat is vastly different from efficient anaerobic training to gain strength. There is really no reason to abandon one in favor of the other. Aerobic training, by definition, is low intensity and of an extended duration. This means that if you are jogging on a treadmill, for example, you should be able to carry on a normal conversation with the person beside you. You should not be gasping for breath or otherwise exerting yourself at a rate that you cannot sustain for 20, 30, or 40 minutes. This type of low-intensity exercise has wonderfully beneficial effects on the heart and respiratory system but does virtually nothing to tax the skeletal muscles. While it can always be argued that the body has a finite recovery capacity and that any exercise other than weight lifting will decrease your rate of progress, as a practical matter I have yet to see a single person arrest his strength training progress by performing proper aerobics three or four days per week.

It should be noted that the progressive intensity that is critical to anaerobic strength training is not a required element of aerobic training. The inability to make this distinction causes some people to engage in "progressive aerobics," which eventually sees them donning 40-pound backpacks and running hills in order to outdo their last effort. That is not proper aerobic training. In aerobics it is entirely appropriate to adopt a program of, say, four 30-minute walks per week and then leave that program unchanged for 20 years. It's only when you turn your aerobic training into a high-intensity effort that it can begin to cause any appreciable decrease in your rate of progress in strength training.

Train Smart,
Pete Sisco & John Little

INDEX

A

Abdominal muscles, 31
Actin filaments, 111–12
Actin proteins, 105, 107
Adenosine diphosphate
    (ADP), 108
Adenosine triphosphate
    (ATP), 107–8
ADP. *See* Adenosine
    diphosphate (ADP)
Aerobic pathways,
    108–9

Aerobic training
    losing body fat and,
        7–8, 144–45
    objective of, 109
Aging, maintaining
    muscles and, 5
Alcoholism, 12
"All or none" principle, of
    muscle fiber contrac-
    tion, 92–93
Amino acids, 117
Anaerobic pathways, 108–9
Anaerobic training, 144–45

Z